Lady Macdonald's
CHOCOLATE
BOOK

Chocolate Mousse Cake (page 48)

Lady Macdonald's

CHOCOLATE
BOOK

Over 70 wickedly delicious recipes
for soufflés, cheesecakes, mousses,
gâteaux and ice creams.

EBURY PRESS LONDON

Published by Ebury Press
Division of The National Magazine Company Ltd
Colquhoun House
27–37 Broadwick Street
London W1V 1FR

First impression 1988

ISBN 0 85223 736 7

Edited by Susan Ward and Helen Dore
Art Direction by Frank Phillips
Photography by James Murphy
Styling by Cathy Sinker
Design by Bill Mason

Phototypeset by Chapterhouse, Formby, L37 3PX
Printed and bound in Italy by New Interlitho, S.p.a., Milan

CONTENTS

INTRODUCTION

'I can't think of anyone better qualified to write a book on chocolate puddings than you,' a friend said to me when I told her what book I was working on. Immodest though it may sound, she is so right. Driven by my passion for all things chocolate I am lucky enough to be able to cook endless puddings of a chocolate nature for our guests here at our home, Kinloch Lodge, which we run as a small hotel. About five nights a week there is a chocolate concoction on the menu – with a fruity alternative, I hasten to add!

I think my passion for chocolate, which is so great that it really could be better described as an addiction, must be inherited from my father and mother, who are similarly afflicted. Indeed, the craving for chocolate is so strong in our family that during the war my aunt is reputed to have been so desperate for a taste of chocolate that she resorted to eating ex-lax!

I feel that the perfect ending to a meal is chocolate in some form or other. Within this book there are many recipes hopefully to inspire you to experiment with chocolate in mousses, pies, cheesecakes (hot and cold), and hot puddings from the comforting nursery variety like Steamed Chocolate Pudding and Dark Chocolate Rice Pudding to the more sophisticated type, like Hot Baked Chocolate Cheesecake and Hot Chocolate and Coffee Soufflé. There are recipes for iced chocolate puddings, chocolate sauces and other sauces which complement chocolate puddings, and there are many recipes for different chocolate cakes, because a really good chocolate cake makes a delicious pudding, when so many people feel guilty about eating cakes with a cup of tea or coffee at other times of the day.

The great thing about chocolate, almost more than any other thing I can think of, is its versatility. Dark, milk or white chocolate combines so well with such a very wide variety of flavours – fruits, like orange, lemon and lime, pineapple, bananas, apples, cherries, raspberries and strawberries (although personally I don't like chocolate combined with the last two fruits; I know that I am in a minority, but to me, the sweetness of the chocolate makes strawberries and raspberries taste sour and kills their flavour – neither complements the other). Chocolate is equally delicious combined with ginger, coffee or mint. Chocolate is also enhanced by alcohol in many guises – brandy, rum and whisky, and a wide range of liqueurs, including all the orange-based ones, coffee-based ones like Kahlūa and Tia Maria, and nutty ones such as Amaretto and Frangelico. Chocolate is delicious with nuts – almonds,

Dark Chocolate and Praline Terrine with Coffee Cream Sauce (pages 13 and 90)

there are a number of delicious chocolatey things which can be made at their convenience and stored in a tin, to serve with a cup of coffee at the end of dinner. For me, no dinner is complete without something sweet (and chocolatey!) at the end of it, and there are recipes in this book for Chocolate Fudge, Chocolate Biscuit Squares, Chocolate Truffles with Angostura Bitters (delicious!) and Dark and White Chocolate-coated Florentines. There are also recipes for Chocolate Oatmeal Crisp Biscuits, which go very well with a smooth mousse, and Dark Chocolate Rice Crispies, good with a fruit compote.

In fact, there are recipes here which will hopefully satisfy all of you who are, like me, complete chocolate fanatics. And I do hope you get almost as much pleasure from making the recipes as you do from eating them!

All the recipes in this book give delicious results – providing, that is, that you use a good chocolate to cook with. I am amazed that some of my friends who are otherwise extremely good cooks use inferior chocolate in cooking, marketed as Cakebrand south of the border and Scotchoc in Scotland. This makes a waste of all the other ingredients you use with it, and the end result of your recipe is not a patch on what it would be if a good chocolate had been used in the first place. In Britain the oldest and best firm of chocolate manufacturers are Terry's of York. This renowned and prestigious company first made chocolate for eating (as opposed to

hazelnuts, pistachios, walnuts and pecans, and coconut. The flavours of all these nuts complements the taste of chocolate so well, and I like the contrasting textures between smooth, chocolatey puds and crunchy nuts. Chocolate puddings are all embellished by whipped cream (which I like flavoured with vanilla), and hot ones, such as Chocolate Fudge Brownies, are delicious with Vanilla Iced Cream.

For busy people who may well not have time to make an actual pudding when entertaining, drinking) over ninety years ago, and Terry's Bitter Chocolate and Plain Bars are the best chocolate made in this country, and the one I recommend for using in the recipes in this book.

Good chocolate is expensive, but so it should be. Sadly, few of us really know how chocolate is made, from the picking of the cocoa bean (which is the seed of the cacao tree) to the transporting back to this country (the cacao tree is a native of South America), the roasting of the beans once home, and the cracking of the roasted beans to separate the 'nib' from the rest. The nib is the part of the bean the manufacturers are after: more than half the content of the nib is fat, and this is the cocoa butter, the 'mass'. The better the chocolate, the higher the percentage of cocoa mass it contains. The chocolate is then refined once more – without this second refining chocolate would have a grainy texture. When you realize that each cacao tree produces only 2.2 kg (5 lb) cocoa beans a year, and that at the moment the world eats more than a million tons of chocolate a year, you can see how many thousands of acres of cacao trees are needed to produce a sufficient quantity. At Terry's of York, various high quality beans are used in the manufacture of their chocolate and the matter of blending these beans to create the Terry flavour is a story in itself. The Terry Chocolate Manager, or *chocolatier*, combines an exact combination of the various types of beans in order to produce the unique Terry flavour. This flavour is assessed empirically each time.

When melting chocolate, the most important thing to remember is not to overheat it. If this happens the chocolate becomes grainy and loses its fluidity and shine. I recommend melting chocolate in a heatproof bowl over a saucepan of very gently simmering hot water; do not allow the bottom of the bowl to touch the water. Another point to remember is that if cold liquid is added to melted chocolate it will thicken or curdle – the cream, liqueur or whatever should always be warm before it is stirred into melted chocolate. If your chocolate is overheated at the melting stage try stirring a small amount of butter into it, which should help.

None of the recipes in this book contain milk chocolate. I don't think it works well in puddings – the flavour isn't dense enough, and it is too sweet.

So my final word is to reiterate as emphatically as I can that the better the dark chocolate you use to cook with, the better the result will be!

CREAMS, MOUSSES AND SOUFFLÉS

To so many people the ideal pud is a chocolate mousse, and there are so many delicious variations on the theme. In some of the recipes in this chapter you will find a contrasting texture between the smooth mousse and another ingredient: for instance, in the Chocolate Amaretto Macaroon Mousse there is a layer of slightly crunchy almond liqueur-flavoured biscuits at the base of the mousse, while the cool bite of crushed peppermint crisps enriches the whole texture of Chocolate and Peppermint Mousse.

If you like, you can serve a fruity concoction to go with one of these mousses – for example, a compote of sliced oranges (with slivers of preserved ginger, if you like) with the Chocolate and Orange Mousse. Cream features in most of these mousse recipes, but it needn't if you would rather leave it out, in which case add an extra egg to the number of eggs listed in the ingredients.

All these mousses can be made a day ahead, and kept in a cool place, ideally a larder, but a fridge will do. I think that chocolate mousses actually improve by being made a day in advance – the flavour seems to intensify.

WHITE CHOCOLATE MOUSSE

SERVES 6
225g (8oz) good-quality white chocolate
50g (2oz) butter
4 large eggs, separated
a few drops of vanilla essence
chocolate rose leaves (see page 93), to decorate

Break the chocolate into a heatproof bowl and put it over a saucepan of hot water (take care not to let the bottom of the bowl touch the water) until the chocolate is melted. Take the bowl off the pan, and stir in the butter, cut into pieces. Whisk the egg yolks, then stir them with the vanilla essence into the chocolate and butter mixture. Leave to cool.

Whisk the egg whites until they are very stiff, and, using a large metal spoon, fold them quickly and thoroughly through the chocolate mixture. Pour into individual glasses or a serving bowl, and leave to set in a cool place for several hours before serving decorated with chocolate rose leaves.

Chocolate and Orange Mousse (page 12)

White Chocolate Mousse (page 9)

CHOCOLATE AND ORANGE MOUSSE

Chocolate and orange is one of the inspired classic flavour combinations.

SERVES 6-8
175 g (6 oz) dark chocolate
4 large eggs, separated
100 g (4 oz) caster sugar
15 g (½ oz) powdered gelatine
juice of 1 orange
45 ml (3 tbsp) orange liqueur, such as Cointreau
finely grated rind of 2 oranges
300 ml (½ pint) double cream
orange shreds

*B*reak the chocolate into a heatproof bowl and put the bowl over a saucepan of gently simmering water (take care not to let the bottom of the bowl touch the water). Heat gently until the chocolate has melted, then remove the bowl from the pan and cool the chocolate for 5 minutes.

Meanwhile, whisk the egg yolks, gradually adding the caster sugar. Continue whisking until the mixture is pale and very thick. Sprinkle the gelatine over the orange juice and liqueur in a small saucepan and heat very gently until the gelatine granules have dissolved completely, then mix the liquid into the yolks and sugar. Stir in the melted chocolate and orange rind.

Whip the cream until it just holds its shape and fold in half, using a large metal spoon. Whisk the egg whites until they are very stiff and using a large metal spoon, fold them quickly and thoroughly through the chocolatey mixture. Pour into glass dishes or a china serving bowl, and leave in a cool place to set. Serve topped with the remaining cream and the orange shreds.

CHOCOLATE AND PEPPERMINT MOUSSE

This delectable mousse is a rich concoction of contrasting flavours and textures.

SERVES 6-8
15 g (½ oz) powdered gelatine
a few drops of peppermint essence
5 large eggs, separated
150 g (5 oz) caster sugar
300 ml (10 fl oz) double cream
75 g (3 oz) good-quality dark chocolate crisp
peppermints coarsely chopped in a food processor or liquidizer

*S*prinkle the gelatine over 60 ml (4 tbsp) water with the peppermint essence in a small saucepan, and heat very gently until the gelatine granules have completely dissolved.

Whisk the egg yolks, gradually adding the caster sugar, until the mixture is pale and very thick. Whisk in the liquid gelatine and leave the mixture in a cool place until it begins to set and will coat the back of a spoon fairly thickly.

Whip the cream until it just holds its shape, then fold in with the chopped peppermint chocolates, and leave again in a cool place for about 10 minutes. Lastly, whisk the egg whites until they are very stiff, and, using a metal spoon fold them quickly and thoroughly through the mousse.

DARK CHOCOLATE AND PRALINE TERRINE

This heavenly, simple pud is wonderful served with Coffee Cream Sauce (page 90).

SERVES 8-10
600 ml (1 pint) single cream
700 ml (1 ½ lb) dark chocolate
50 ml (2 fl oz) brandy
15 g (2 fl oz) powdered gelatine
5 large egg yolks

For the praline
100 g (4 oz) granulated sugar
50 g (2 oz) flaked almonds

Start by making the praline. Put the sugar and flaked almonds in a heavy-based saucepan over a moderate heat. Shake the pan occasionally – the sugar will take its time melting and it is worth not trying to hurry this, as the melted sugar caramelizes quickly and can so easily burn. Shaking the pan helps the sugar to melt evenly. As the sugar is heating up and melting, thoroughly butter a baking tray. When the sugar is melted and golden-brown and the almonds are golden-brown too, pour the mixture onto the prepared baking tray, and leave until cold. Then put the praline between two sheets of non-stick baking parchment and bash with a rolling pin until reduced to the consistency of coarse crumbs. Store in an airtight container.

To make the terrine: put the cream into a saucepan and heat to just below boiling. Break the chocolate into a food processor. Mix the brandy with 75 ml (3 fl oz) water in a small pan and sprinkle over the gelatine. Heat very gently until the gelatine has dissolved completely.

Pour the hot cream on to the broken-up chocolate in a food processor, put the lid on and cover the lid with a tea-towel. Whizz until the chocolate has melted, then, still whizzing, add the egg yolks one by one. Then pour in the liquid gelatine mixture. Whizz until smoothly incorporated.

Line the base and narrow ends of a 900 g (2 lb) terrine or loaf tin with a strip of non-stick baking parchment, and pour in half the chocolate mixture. Leave in a cool place until thick, then sprinkle with a thick layer of praline. Warm the remaining chocolate mixture, or keep it in a bowl over a saucepan of hot water to prevent it from cooling and setting. Pour over the praline and leave in a cool place for several hours until set.

Dip in a bowl of hot water and count to 5, then run a palette knife round the sides and turn the terrine out onto a serving plate. Cut into slices about 1 cm (½ inch) thick to serve, and serve with Coffee Cream Sauce (page 90).

ORANGE AND CHOCOLATE BAVARIAN CREAM

The flavours of orange and chocolate go so well together in this soft-creamy-textured set custard mixture. I like to decorate the top of this version of a bavarois with crystallized primroses (see page 94) or fine slivers of orange peel arranged in a circle round the sides.

SERVES 6
300 ml (½ pint) milk
150 g (5 oz) dark chocolate
5 ml (1 tsp) powdered gelatine
30 ml (2 tbsp) orange liqueur
4 large egg yolks
100 g (4 oz) caster sugar
grated rind of 2 oranges
300 ml (½ pint) double cream
crystallized primroses or slivers of orange peel to
decorate

*P*ut the milk into a saucepan with the chocolate broken into bits. Heat gently until the chocolate has melted. Meanwhile, sprinkle the gelatine over the liqueur and 30 ml (2 tbsp) cold water in a small saucepan, then heat very gently until the gelatine granules have dissolved completely.

Whisk the egg yolks, gradually adding the sugar. Whisk until the mixture is very thick and pale. Pour on a little of the hot chocolate milk and mix well with the yolks, then pour back into the saucepan containing the remaining chocolate milk. Stir continuously over a gentle to moderate heat (do not boil) until the mixture coats the back of the spoon. Then remove the pan from the heat and stir in the grated orange rind, and the liquid gelatine, stirring until the gelatine has dissolved completely in the hot custard.

Leave the custard to cool completely, stirring occasionally to prevent a skin from forming. When it is quite cold, whip the cream until it just holds its shape, then fold into the custard. Pour into a glass or china serving dish and leave in a cool place to set. Decorate with crystallised primroses or slivers of orange peel. Leave in a cool place until you are ready to serve it.

Orange and Chocolate Bavarian Cream, Dark and White Chocolate-coated Florentines (pages 14 and 81)

CHOCOLATE AMARETTO MACAROON MOUSSE

Amaretto biscuits are widely available from good delicatessens. They can enhance many a pud, but especially this mousse; the crunch of the crushed amaretti punctuating its smooth creaminess.

SERVES 6-8
150 g (5 oz) dark chocolate, broken up
100 g (4 oz) amaretto biscuits, available from most delicatessens
45 ml (3 tbsp) Amaretto liqueur
4 large eggs, separated
150 g (5 oz) caster sugar
150 ml (¼ pint) double cream

*P*ut the chocolate into a heatproof bowl over a saucepan of hot water (take care not to let the bottom of the bowl touch the water) until the chocolate has melted.

Break up the amaretti by crunching them in your hands, and put them into the bottom of a serving bowl. Sprinkle the Amaretto liqueur over the broken-up biscuits.

Whisk the egg yolks, gradually adding the caster sugar, and continue whisking until the mixture is pale and very thick. Fold in the melted chocolate and leave until the mixture is quite cold, then fold in the cream whipped until it just holds its shape. Lastly, whisk the whites until they are very stiff and, using a large metal spoon, fold them quickly and thoroughly through the chocolate mousse. Pour the mixture on top of the amaretti in the serving bowl.

As your guests help themselves to this mousse, remember to ask them to dig down with the spoon so that they get some of the delicious almondy biscuits at the bottom!

HOT CHOCOLATE AND COFFEE SOUFFLÉ

This soufflé of chocolate, its flavour enhanced with coffee, is really one of my favourite puddings. A hot soufflé makes an elegant finale to a meal. I like to serve a sauce with a soufflé, in this case Coffee Cream Sauce (page 90).

SERVES 6
300 ml (½ pint) milk
15 g (½ oz) cornflour
12 ml (2 rounded tsp) instant coffee
6 large eggs, separated
100 g (4 oz) caster sugar
225 g (8 oz) good-quality dark chocolate, broken into a bowl and melted over a saucepan of gently simmering water
15 ml (1 tbsp) icing sugar, to finish

*B*utter a large soufflé dish – about 20 cm (8 inch) in diameter – and dust it with a spoonful of caster sugar. Stir a spoonful of the milk into the cornflour. Heat the rest of the milk and the coffee granules in a saucepan. Add some of the hot milky coffee to the cornflour mixture. Stir well, then beat this into the coffee-flavoured milk in the saucepan. Stir until the sauce boils.

In a bowl, beat the egg yolks well, gradually adding the caster sugar. Beat in the melted chocolate and, lastly, the cooled coffee and cornflour mixture. In another bowl, whisk the egg whites until they are very stiff. Using a large metal spoon, fold them quickly and thoroughly into the chocolate mixture. Pour this into the prepared soufflé dish and bake in the oven pre-heated to 200°C (400°F/Gas Mark 6), or the top oven in a four-door Aga for 35–40 minutes.

Have a spoonful of icing sugar and a sieve ready to hand. When the cooking time is up, take the soufflé out of the oven, quickly dust it with the icing sugar, and serve it immediately, accompanied by the Coffee Cream Sauce.

MOCHA MOUSSE

This is another classic flavour combination. But whereas rich chocolate and sweetly acid orange contrast with each other so deliciously, here chocolate is enhanced and made subtly deeper in flavour by the coffee.

SERVES 6-8
15 g (½ oz) powdered gelatine
60 ml (4 tbsp) water
175 g (6 oz) dark chocolate, broken up
10 ml (2 tsp) good-quality instant coffee, eg Gold Blend, dissolved in 30 ml (2 tbsp) boiling water
4 large eggs, separated
100 g (4 oz) caster sugar
300 ml (10 fl oz) double cream

Sprinkle the gelatine over 60 ml (4 tbsp) water in a small saucepan. Heat very gently until dissolved completely.

Put the broken chocolate and the dissolved coffee into a heatproof bowl over a saucepan of hot water (take care not to let the bottom of the bowl touch the water) until the chocolate has melted. Carefully stir the melted chocolate and the coffee liquid together.

Whisk the egg yolks, gradually adding the caster sugar and continuing to whisk until the mixture is very pale and thick. Stir in the melted chocolate and coffee, and the liquid gelatine, and leave to cool. Then fold in half the cream whipped until it just holds its shape. Lastly, whisk the egg whites until they are very stiff, and, using a large metal spoon, fold them quickly and thoroughly through the mousse. Pour into a serving bowl and leave for several hours, then cover with the remaining whipped cream.

If you like, you can whip the cream until it is stiff enough to pipe in rosettes around the edge of the mousse, and if you can get them, decorate the rosettes with dark chocolate coffee beans. If you make the mousse a day in advance, don't decorate it with the whipped cream, piped or otherwise, until a couple of hours before serving.

MERINGUE PUDDINGS

*C*hocolate and meringue is a heavenly combination. In this chapter there are recipes for chocolate with all sorts of different meringues: nutty-flavoured with chocolate cream; chocolate-flavoured; coffee with rich chocolate and coffee butter-cream (this must be one of the richest recipes in this book, but also one of the most delicious); and a chocolate meringue gâteau with black cherries and cream.

Meringue is so convenient, because it can usually be made several days in advance and stored in an airtight tin. In some cases the entire pudding can be made and frozen, as in the Cherry and Chocolate Cream Meringue Gâteau.

VANILLA AND CHOCOLATE CREAM PAVLOVA

A favourite combination of soft vanilla meringue, whipped cream and dark chocolate.

SERVES 8
4 large egg whites
225g (8oz) caster sugar
5ml (1 tsp) cornflour, sieved
5ml (1 tsp) white wine vinegar
5ml (1 tsp) vanilla essence

For the decoration
300ml (½ pint) double cream
175g (6oz) dark chocolate, coarsely grated

*L*ine a baking tray with non-stick baking parchment. Mark a large circle or a square or rectangle if you prefer.

Whisk the egg whites until they are stiff, then, still whisking, add the caster sugar a spoonful at a time, until all the sugar is incorporated and you have a stiff meringue. Using a large metal spoon, fold in the cornflour, vinegar and vanilla essence. Smooth the meringue into the desired shape on the prepared baking tray, and bake in the oven pre-heated to 180°C (350°F/Gas Mark 4) for 5 minutes, then at 110°C (225°F/Gas Mark ¼), or the top left oven in a four-door Aga, for a further 45 minutes. Take the meringue out of the oven and leave to cool completely on the baking tray.

When the pavlova is quite cold (you can make it in the morning for dinner in the evening) carefully put it on a serving plate or tray, and cover with cream, whipped until fairly stiff. (I don't add any sugar to the whipped cream because even I, with my sweet teeth, don't think this pudding needs it.) Then sprinkle with the grated dark chocolate.

Vanilla and Chocolate Cream Pavlova (page 18)

CHOCOLATE AND CHESTNUT CREAM MERINGUE

In this luscious pud chocolate-flavoured meringue is made by whisking together the egg whites and the icing sugar in a bowl over heat. The cocoa powder is then sieved in, and the meringue shaped into two large rounds then baked. The finished meringue is sandwiched together with whipped cream mixed with sweetened chestnut purée, and the top of the meringue is decorated with whipped cream and dark chocolate caraque. To really gild the lily, you can also pipe rosettes of whipped cream round the sides of the meringue, and put a quarter of a marron glacé on each rosette.

SERVES 6-8
4 large egg whites
225 g (8 oz) icing sugar, sieved
25 g (1 oz) cocoa powder
vanilla essence
300 ml (½ pint) double cream
225 g (8 oz) can sweetened chestnut purée
50 g (2 oz) dark chocolate caraque (see page 93)
150 ml (¼ pint) extra double cream, whipped (optional)

To make the meringue, put the egg whites into a heatproof bowl and add the icing sugar. Put the bowl over a saucepan of gently simmering water and whisk for several minutes until the mixture becomes a thick meringue (this is most easily done with a hand-held electric whisk). Take the bowl off the heat and fold in the sieved cocoa.

Line two baking trays with non-stick baking parchment and measure out a circle about 23 cm (9 inch) on each. (I use a plate.) Divide the meringue mixture evenly between the two and smooth into rounds. Bake in the oven pre-heated to 110°C (225°F/Gas Mark ¼), or the top right oven in a four-door Aga, for 2½–3 hours. Cool the meringues and store in an airtight container.

To finish, whizz the chestnut purée in a food processor, or put it into a bowl and break it down with the back of a wooden spoon against the sides of the bowl, to get as smooth a purée as you can. (If you can't get sweetened chestnut purée, add 25 g (1 oz) caster sugar to the purée.) Flavour with a few drops of vanilla essence. Fold in all but a large spoonful of the cream, whipped until fairly stiff and spread the remaining spoonful of whipped cream over the surface. Sprinkle with the chocolate caraque. If you like, pipe rosettes round the edge of the meringue gâteau, using the extra cream.

For easier slicing, a serrated knife, dipped into a jug of very hot water is invaluable! Fill the meringue two or three hours before serving, and keep in a cool place.

COFFEE, CHOCOLATE AND ALMOND MERINGUE GÂTEAU

As I said in the introduction to this chapter, this is probably the richest recipe in this book – a yummy concoction combining coffee-flavoured meringue with a rich coffee- and chocolate-flavoured buttercream filling and covering. It is covered with toasted flaked almonds, which provide a delicious combination of flavours as well as a good contrasting crunch. It has the added bonus of being much better made the day before it is to be eaten.

SERVES 8

For the meringue
4 large egg whites
225 g (8 oz) caster sugar
10 ml (2 tsp) instant coffee dissolved in 30 ml (2 tbsp)
*   boiling water, then cooled*

For the filling
225 g (8 oz) unsalted butter
225 g (8 oz) icing sugar, sieved
4 egg yolks
100 g (4 oz) dark chocolate, melted with 10 ml (2 tsp)
*   instant coffee dissolved in 30 ml (2 tbsp) hot water*
75 g (3 oz) flaked almonds, toasted until golden-
*   brown*

To make the meringue, first line two baking trays with non-stick baking parchment. Mark out a circle about 23 cm (9 inch) on each circle – I use a plate to draw round. Put the egg whites into a clean bowl and whisk until stiff, then, still whisking, gradually add the caster sugar a spoonful at a time. Whisk until all the sugar is incorporated and you have a stiff meringue. Using a large metal spoon, quickly fold in the cold coffee liquid, then divide the meringue between the two circles. Smooth into rounds and bake in the oven pre-heated to 110°C (225°F/Gas Mark ¼) or the top left oven in a four door Aga, for 2½–3 hours, then cool.

To make the filling, beat the butter, gradually adding the icing sugar a spoonful at a time and beating until the mixture is pale and soft. Beat in the egg yolks one at a time, alternating with the cooled melted chocolate and coffee mixture.

Sandwich the meringue rounds together with about half of this buttercream, then spread the top and sides of the gâteau with the remaining buttercream. Cover the surface with the toasted flaked almonds, and leave the gâteau in a cool place overnight, until you are ready to serve it. To help slice it evenly, a serrated knife dipped into a jug of very hot water is invaluable.

Chocolate and Chestnut Cream Meringue (page 20)

Coffee, Chocolate and Almond Meringue Gâteau (page 21)

CHERRY AND CHOCOLATE MERINGUE GÂTEAU

This is one of those finished meringue puddings which freezes very successfully.

SERVES 6-8
4 large egg whites
225 g (8 oz) icing sugar, sieved
25 g (1 oz) cocoa powder

For the filling
300 ml (½ pint) double cream
30 ml (2 tbsp) Kirsch (optional)
425 g (15 oz) can stoned black cherries, well-drained
50 g (2 oz) dark chocolate, grated
15 ml (1 tbsp) icing sugar, sieved
150 ml (¼ pint) extra double cream

𝒯o make the meringue, put the egg whites and the icing sugar into a heatproof bowl over a saucepan of gently simmering water, and whisk for several minutes until the meringue is very thick. Take the bowl off the heat and fold in the sieved cocoa powder.

Line two baking trays with non-stick baking parchment and mark a circle about 23 cm (9 inch) on each – I use a plate to draw round. Divide the chocolate meringue mixture between the rounds, and smooth it out evenly. Bake in the oven pre-heated to 110°C (225°F/Gas Mark ¼), or the top left oven in a four-door Aga, for 2½–3 hours, then remove the meringues from the oven and leave to cool.

Fold together the cream, whipped until fairly stiff, and Kirsch, if used, the drained cherries and grated chocolate, and spread over the top of one of the meringue rounds. Cover with the other round and dust with icing sugar. If you like, use the extra cream, whipped stiffly, to pipe rosettes round the edge of the gâteau. To serve, have a serrated knife dipped in a jug of very hot water to hand – it makes for a much easier job when cutting this delicious gâteau.

If you are going to freeze the gâteau, cover it carefully and freeze, without the dusting of icing sugar; add this just before serving. To thaw, allow 3–4 hours at room temperature.

HAZELNUT MERINGUE WITH CHOCOLATE CREAM

In this pudding there is a chocolate and nut combination again, but giving a totally different result. This time the meringue is made with ground hazelnuts, and the chocolate flavouring is in the whipped cream filling. The surface of the meringue is dusted with a mixture of icing sugar and cocoa powder, sieved together, and rosettes of whipped cream are piped round the edges of the gâteau.

SERVES 6-8
For the meringue
4 large egg whites
225g (8oz) caster sugar
5ml (1 tsp) white wine vinegar
5ml (1 tsp) vanilla essence
100g (4oz) ground hazelnuts, toasted until golden, then cooled

For the filling and decoration
450ml (¾ pint) double cream
75g (3oz) dark chocolate, melted
10ml (2tsp) icing sugar
1ml (2tsp) cocoa powder

To make the meringue, put the egg whites into a clean bowl and whisk until fairly stiff. Then, still whisking, add the caster sugar a spoonful at a time, whisking until all the sugar is incorporated and you have a stiff meringue. Add the vinegar and vanilla essence, and fold them and the ground hazelnuts through the meringue, using a large metal spoon.

Divide the meringue mixture between two 20 cm (8 inch) sandwich cake tins base-lined with non-stick baking parchment. Smooth the tops and bake in the oven pre-heated to 180°C (350°F/Gas Mark 4), or the bottom right oven in a four-door Aga, for 35 minutes. Take the meringues out of the oven, leave in the tins for 5 minutes, then turn out carefully onto a wire rack to cool. The meringues will have a crusty surface which may crack and crumble a bit – don't worry.

For the filling, reserve about one-third of the fairly stiff whipped cream for piping the rosettes. Carefully fold the cooled melted chocolate into the remaining cream. Spread this over the top of one of the meringue rounds. Cover with the remaining meringue and sieve the icing sugar mixed with the cocoa powder over the surface. Pipe rosettes of the remaining whipped cream at intervals round the edges.

Fill and decorate the gâteau not much more than an hour before serving, and again, to make the cutting easier, a serrated knife dipped into a jug of very hot water is the answer!

CHOCOLATE MERINGUES WITH RUM-WHIPPED CREAM

These meringues are foolproof – they are 'cooked' as they are made, by whisking the egg whites and the icing sugar together over heat. The cocoa powder is then folded into the thick meringue: don't be tempted to whisk the cocoa into the egg whites together with the icing sugar, or the meringue simply won't thicken. These meringues can be stored in an airtight container for several days, and sandwiched together with the rum-flavoured whipped cream two or three hours before serving.

SERVES 6
4 large egg whites
225 g (8 oz) icing sugar, sieved
25 g (1 oz) cocoa powder
a few drops of vanilla essence
300 ml (½ pint) double cream
60 ml (4 tbsp) white or dark rum
100 g (4 oz) dark chocolate

Put the egg whites into a heatproof bowl over a saucepan of simmering water. Add the icing sugar and whisk (this is most easily done with a hand-held electric whisk) for several minutes until the mixture becomes very thick. Then take the bowl off the heat, sieve the cocoa powder over the meringue in the bowl, and fold this and the vanilla essence through the meringue, using a large metal spoon.

Line a large baking tray with non-stick baking parchment and pipe even-sized meringues on to it. To serve 6 people you need 12 meringues, so aim to pipe meringues about 5 cm (2 inches) in diameter. For an especially pretty result, use a large star shaped nozzle.

Bake the meringues in the oven pre-heated to 110°C (225°F/Gas Mark ¼) or the top left oven in a four door Aga, for about 3 hours. Take the meringues out of the oven, lift them off the paper and cool completely on a wire rack. When they are completely cold, store them in an airtight container.

Two or three hours before serving, whip the cream until stiff, gradually adding the rum. Coarsely grate the chocolate then fold into the cream. Use to sandwich the meringues together. I think they look decorative served piled up on a small cake stand.

Chocolate Meringues with Rum-whipped Cream (page 26)

ICED CREAMS

*C*hocolate iced creams come in a variety of wonderful flavour combinations. In this chapter there are recipes for chestnut and chocolate iced cream – a smooth chocolate iced cream with pieces of marron glacé in it – and for Chocolate and Peppermint Crisp Iced Cream, a universal favourite with children and adults alike. There is a Christmassy recipe for Nesselrode iced cream, and a rich chocolate iced cream containing raisins soaked in rum. There are two iced cream recipes which aren't chocolatey in themselves, but both are so delicious served with a Dark Chocolate Sauce (see page 92) that I felt they belonged here!

CHOCOLATE AND PEPPERMINT CRISP ICED CREAM

Use top-quality peppermint crisp chocolates for the finest result.

SERVES 8
4 large eggs, separated
100g (4 oz) icing sugar, sieved
7.5 ml (1 ½ tsp) cocoa powder
300 ml (½ pint) double cream
225 g (8 oz) dark chocolate peppermint crisps

*W*hisk the egg whites until they are stiff, then, still whisking continuously, add the icing sugar, a spoonful at a time, until you have a thick meringue. Next, whip the cream, then whisk the egg yolks until they are pale and slightly thickened. Whisk the cocoa into the yolks, then fold into the cream. Fold into the meringue mixture.

Very finely chop the chocolate peppermint crisps in a blender or food processor, a few at a time, and fold them through the mixture. Pour into a container, cover and freeze.

There is no need to beat this iced cream half-way through freezing. Leave it at room temperature 30 minutes before serving.

CHOCOLATE AND MARRONS GLACÉ ICED CREAM

This is one of my favourite chocolatey iced creams. The contrast in texture between the smooth, rich iced cream and the pieces of marron glacé is quite delicious.

SERVES 6-8
75 g (3 oz) caster sugar
175 g (6 oz) dark chocolate
4 large egg yolks
300 ml (½ pint) double cream
8 marrons glacés

*P*ut the sugar into a saucepan with 90 ml (6 tbsp) water. Heat gently without letting the liquid boil, until the sugar has dissolved completely, then boil fast for 3 minutes.

Meanwhile, break the chocolate into a blender or food processor. Pour the hot sugar syrup straight onto the chocolate, put the lid on and whizz – the noise will be horrendous but the chocolate soon melts in the heat of the syrup. Still whizzing, add the egg yolks. Leave to cool, then fold into the cream, whipped until it just holds its shape. Cut the marrons glacés into chunks and fold them through, then freeze.

Leave for 20 minutes at room temperature to soften slightly before serving.

VANILLA ICED CREAM

This is the best recipe I know for vanilla ice – it is invaluable, because it doesn't need beating halfway through its freezing time. The recipe was given to me many years ago by a great friend, Caroline Fox, and I am eternally grateful to her for it. Vanilla Iced Cream is so good with Chocolate Sauce (page 92), but it also enhances many chocolate puddings, especially hot ones, like Pears with Hot Chocolate Sauce (page 76), and Chocolate Fudge Brownies (page 72).

SERVES 6-8
4 large eggs, separated
100 g (4 oz) icing sugar, sieved
300 ml (½ pint) double cream
2.5 ml (½ tsp) vanilla essence

*W*hisk the egg whites until they are stiff, then add the icing sugar a teaspoonful at a time, whisking continuously until all the sugar is incorporated and you have a very stiff meringue.

Quickly (and using the same whisk) whip the cream with the vanilla essence until it just holds its shape. Lastly, whisk the egg yolks until they are paler in colour and slightly thickened. Then, using a large metal spoon, fold the yolks into the cream, and then the meringue mixture into the cream and yolks. Pour into a container, cover and freeze. Remove from the freezer 30 minutes before serving and leave at room temperature to soften slightly.

ICED CHOCOLATE AND BRANDY CREAMS

These little ramekins of rich, dense, chocolate cream are very convenient – they can be eaten straight from the freezer. The brandy in them prevents the cream from freezing rock hard.

MAKES 8 SMALL RAMEKINS
300 ml (½ pint) double cream
175 g (6 oz) dark chocolate
3 large egg yolks
45 ml (3 tbsp) honey, heated until very hot
45 ml (3 tbsp) brandy
White chocolate leaves (see page 93)

*P*ut the cream into a saucepan and break the chocolate into it. Over a gentle heat, melt the chocolate in the cream, stirring until both cream and chocolate are well combined.

Take the saucepan off the heat and cool the cream mixture. It will thicken as it cools, so take care not to let it become too stiff to fold into the yolk mixture. Put the egg yolks into a bowl and pour on the hot honey, whisking vigorously with an electric whisk. Continue whisking until the yolks become very pale and thick, then whisk in the brandy.

Fold together the chocolate cream and the yolk and honey mixtures, and divide among the ramekins. Open-freeze the ramekins on a tray, then when they are quite hard, cover each ramekin and freeze. Serve decorated with chocolate leaves.

ORANGE AND LEMON ICED CREAM

This is another iced cream which is sublime when served with a warm chocolate sauce. It does need a good beating halfway through freezing – or if you have an ice-cream machine you can freeze-churn it in that.

SERVES 6-8
8 large egg yolks (make meringues with the whites)
225 g (8 oz) caster sugar
grated rind of 2 lemons
grated rind of 2 oranges
juice of 1 lemon
300 ml (½ pint) double cream
juice of 1 orange

*W*hisk the egg yolks until they are pale, gradually adding the sugar. Continue whisking until the mixture is very thick. Whisk in the lemon and orange rind, and the lemon juice.

Whip the cream until it just holds its shape, gradually whipping in the orange juice. Fold together the egg yolk and cream mixtures, mixing them thoroughly. Pour into a container, cover and freeze. After a couple of hours in the freezer, take the iced cream out, scrape the frozen sides into the middle and whisk well with an electric whisk. Re-freeze until needed. Leave the iced cream at room temperature for 30 minutes before serving with Dark Chocolate Sauce (page 92).

Iced Chocolate and Brandy Creams (page 30)

RICH CHOCOLATE, RAISIN AND RUM ICED CREAM

This basic chocolate iced cream recipe is the best I know but I can't claim credit for it because it is the invention of Katie Stewart who very kindly let me include it in my book *Sweet Things*. I have to say that the addition of the raisins and booze is my idea!

SERVES 6-8
75g (3oz) raisins
90ml (6 tbsp) white or dark rum
225g (8oz) dark chocolate
75g (3oz) caster sugar
4 large egg yolks
300ml (½ pint) double cream

Soak the raisins in the rum for as long as possible – overnight is best, in a bowl covered with clingfilm: when you take off the clingfilm the fumes will knock you out for a second or two!

Break the chocolate into a blender or food processor. Measure 90 ml (6 tbsp) water into a saucepan and add the caster sugar. Over a gentle heat, dissolve the sugar in the water, then boil fast for 3 minutes. Pour the hot sugar syrup onto the chocolate, cover the lid of the blender or processor with a tea-towel, and whizz for several seconds – the noise will be rather alarming but never fear, it doesn't last for long.

When the mixture is quite smooth, add the yolks, one by one and whizz until they are smoothly incorporated. Leave the chocolate mixture to cool.

Meanwhile, whip the cream until it just holds its shape, whipping in any unsoaked-up rum from the raisins. Fold the raisins into the cream, then fold together the cream and raisin mixture and the chocolate mixture. Pour into a polythene container, cover and freeze.

Take the iced cream out of the freezer about 30 minutes before serving, and leave it at room temperature.

ICED CHOCOLATE NESSELRODE PUDDING

This makes a good alternative to traditional Christmas pudding if it is frozen in a pudding basin, then dipped in hot water for a few seconds before unmoulding on to a serving plate. It is also delicious eaten at *any* time of the year! I love the contrasting textures of the boozy fruit and cruncy almonds in the smooth chocolate cream.

SERVES 8
100 g (4 oz) seedless raisins
50 g (2 oz) dried apricots, chopped
60 ml (4 tbsp) brandy
300 ml (½ pint) single cream
100 g (4 oz) dark chocolate
4 large egg yolks
75 g (3 oz) caster sugar
300 ml (½ pint) double cream
*50 g (2 oz) flaked almonds, toasted until golden, then
    cooled*
*200 g (7 oz) can whole unsweetened chestnuts,
    drained and broken up*
dried apricots and gold almond dragees

The day before, put the raisins and apricots into a shallow dish and cover with the brandy. Cover the dish with clingfilm and leave overnight.

Next day, put the single cream into a saucepan and break the chocolate into it. Melt the chocolate in the cream over a gentle heat. Beat together the egg yolks and caster sugar, and pour the hot cream and chocolate mixture on to the yolk mixture. Mix well, pour back into the saucepan, and, over a moderate heat, stir until the mixture coats the back of the wooden spoon. Take the pan off the heat and cool, stirring occasionally to prevent a skin forming.

Whip the double cream until it just holds its shape, then fold in the raisins, apricots, toasted almonds and pieces of chestnut. When the chocolate mixture is completely cold, fold it into the cream and fruit mixture, and pour into a polythene container or a pudding bowl to freeze. Remove from the freezer, unmould and leave for 30 minutes at room temperature before serving, decorated with dried apricots and gold almond dragees, if desired.

33

Iced Chocolate Nesselrode Pudding (page 33)

Rich Chocolate, Raisin and Rum Iced Cream (page 32)

CAKES AND GÂTEAUX

Most people love cakes, but guilt usually prevents them from indulging their passion by eating cake in the traditional way with a cup of tea or coffee. I love making gooey cake concoctions to serve as a pudding and in this chapter there are lots of recipes for cake and chocolate combinations. Somehow nutty cakes and chocolate go very well together, so I have included recipes using nuts of all sorts. In many cases, the actual cake part of the recipes can be made and frozen, and the cake then filled and covered before serving.

CHOCOLATE AND ALMOND CAKE

This very simple, very rich cake makes a delicious pudding. I like to serve it with cream, whipped until it just holds its shape, flavoured with vanilla, or with Vanilla Iced Cream (page 29). Unlike most cake recipes where you are told to stick a skewer or knife into the centre of the cake to test whether the cake is cooked if the skewer comes out clean, in this one the cake is ready when the skewer comes out with some of the cake sticking to it, as it should be slightly gooey and moist.

SERVES 8-10
225 g (8 oz) butter
225 g (8 oz) soft light brown sugar
225 g (8 oz) dark chocolate, melted
5 ml (1 tsp) vanilla essence
6 large eggs
225 g (8 oz) ground almonds, sieved
15 ml (1 tbsp) icing sugar, sieved

Butter a 22.5 cm (9 inch) springform cake tin and line the base with non-stick baking parchment.

In a mixing bowl, cream the butter, gradually adding the sugar. Beat until the mixture is soft and fluffy. Beat in the cooled melted chocolate, vanilla essence, and the eggs, one by one, beating well after each addition. Lastly, fold in the ground almonds. Pour the cake mixture into the prepared tin. Bake in the oven pre-heated to 180°C (350°F/Gas Mark 4), or the bottom right oven in four-door Aga, for 35–40 minutes. (When a skewer is inserted into the centre of the cake, some of the cake mixture should stick to it.)

Remove the cake from the oven and allow to cool completely in its tin. Turn it out, when cold, on to a serving plate, and dust with the icing sugar. Hand a bowl of whipped vanilla-flavoured cream, or a dish of Vanilla Iced Cream (page 29) to serve with the slices of dark, moist cake.

CHOCOLATE AND ORANGE CAKE

This is a really fudgey-textured cake, flavoured with orange, and with a chocolate fudge icing. It is very simple to make, but so good!

SERVES 8

For the cake
175g (6oz) butter
175g (6oz) soft light brown sugar
75g (3oz) self-raising flour
225g (8oz) drinking chocolate powder
4 large eggs
grated rind and juice of 1 orange

For the filling
100g (4oz) butter
100g (4oz) icing sugar, sieved
grated rind of 1 orange

For the icing
50g (2oz) butter
50g (2oz) granulated sugar
juice of 1 orange
175g (6oz) icing sugar
25g (1oz) cocoa powder

*B*utter two 20 cm (8 inch) sandwich tins and line the base of each with a disc of non-stick baking parchment. To make the cake, cream the butter in a bowl, gradually adding the sugar. Beat really well until the mixture is soft and fluffy, then sieve together the flour and drinking chocolate powder. Beat the eggs into the creamed mixture, alternately with spoonfuls of the sieved flour and drinking chocolate mixture. When it is all incorporated, beat in the orange rind and juice. Pour the mixture into the two prepared tins and bake in the oven pre-heated to 180°C (350°F/Gas Mark 4), or the bottom right oven in a four-door Aga, for 30 minutes. Remove the cakes from the oven and leave to cool in their tins for a few minutes before turning them on to wire racks. Leave until completely cold.

Meanwhile, make the orange buttercream for the filling: cream the butter in a bowl, gradually adding the icing sugar and orange rind. Beat until light and fluffy.

To make the icing, put the butter, granulated sugar, orange juice and 30 ml (2 tbsp) of water into a saucepan. Heat gently until the butter has melted and the sugar completely dissolved, then boil fast for 5 minutes. Sieve the icing sugar and cocoa together into a bowl, and beat in the boiled orange syrup. Beat from time to time until cool, thick and glossy.

To assemble the cake, put one of the cakes on a serving plate and spread the buttercream evenly over the top. Put the remaining cake on top. Cover the top and sides of the cake with the icing. If you like, arrange pieces of crystallized orange peel around the edge of the top of the cake, either in a continuous circle, or in evenly spaced clusters.

SACHERTORTE

There are many variations of this famous rich chocolate cake, originally the creation of a master baker in Vienna. By tradition it has a chocolate fondant icing, but the icing here gives a smooth and glossy finish. By custom, the name 'Sacher' is piped across the top.

SERVES 8-10

For the cake
175 g (6 oz) plain chocolate
150 g (5 oz) unsalted butter
150 g (5 oz) caster sugar
5 ml (1 tsp) vanilla essence
6 large eggs, separated
200 g (7 oz) ground almonds
25 g (1 oz) cornflour

For the glaze
100 g (4 oz) apricot jam

For the icing
225 g (8 oz) plain chocolate, broken up
225 ml (8 fl oz) double cream

First make the cake. Butter a 25 cm (10 inch) springform cake tin and line the base with a disc of non-stick baking parchment. To make the cake, break the chocolate into a heatproof bowl set over a saucepan of gently simmering water (take care that the bottom of the bowl does not touch the water). Heat gently until the chocolate melts. Take the bowl off the heat and stir until the chocolate is smooth.

In a bowl, cream the butter, gradually adding half the sugar. Beat until the mixture is soft and pale. Gradually beat in the vanilla essence and egg yolks alternately with the melted chocolate.

Whisk the egg whites until they are fairly stiff, then, still whisking, gradually incorporate the remaining sugar. Using a large metal spoon thoroughly and quickly fold in the whisked egg white and sugar mixture alternately with the ground almonds sieved with the cornflour. Pour the mixture into the prepared cake tin, scraping down the sides of the bowl. Bake in the oven pre-heated to 180°C (350°F/Gas Mark 4), or the bottom right oven in a four-door Aga, for 40–50 minutes, or until a skewer pushed into the centre of the cake comes out clean. Remove the cake from the oven and leave to cool in its tin.

When cold, turn the cake on to a serving plate, and peel off the lining paper. Heat the apricot jam for the glaze until boiling. Brush over the top and sides of the cake and leave until cold.

To make the icing, simply break the chocolate into a heatproof bowl, add the cream, and set the bowl over a saucepan of gently simmering water until the chocolate has melted (take care that the bottom of the bowl does not touch the water). Take the bowl off the pan, stir the mixture gently, then pour over the cake. Gently shake the cake to spread the chocolate cream icing evenly – if necessary use a palette knife to make sure the cake is smoothly and completely covered. Leave in a cool place to set – do not refrigerate.

Sachertorte (page 38)

DEVIL'S FOOD CAKE WITH AMERICAN FROSTING

As with the Sachertorte, there are many variations of Devil's Food Cake. Sometimes it is iced with a chocolate buttercream, but I like it best iced with a stiff white American frosting. I love the contrast of the fluffy meringue-like icing with the dark chocolate cake.

SERVES 8
For the cake
175 g (6 oz) butter
175 g (6 oz) soft light brown sugar
100 g (4 oz) dark chocolate
225 g (8 oz) self-raising flour
5 ml (1 tsp) bicarbonate of soda
2.5 ml (½ tsp) salt
150 ml (¼ pint) milk
5 ml (1 tsp) vanilla essence
2 large eggs

For the frosting
450 g (1 lb) granulated sugar
150 ml (¼ pint) water
a few drops of vanilla essence
2 egg whites

Butter two 22.5 cm (9 inch) sandwich cake tins, and line the base of each with a disc of non-stick baking parchment. To make the cake, break the chocolate into a heatproof bowl and set over a saucepan of gently simmering water (take care that the bottom of the bowl does not touch the water). Heat gently until the chocolate has melted.

Cream the butter in a bowl, gradually adding the sugar, and beat until the mixture is fluffy. Sieve together the flour, soda and salt, and beat this into the creamed mixture, alternately with the milk and vanilla essence. Beat in the eggs, one by one, then the cooled melted chocolate.

Divide the mixture between the two prepared tins and smooth out evenly. Bake in the oven pre-heated to 180°C (350°F/Gas Mark 4) or the bottom right oven in a four-door Aga, for 30–35 minutes, until a skewer inserted into the centre of the cakes comes out clean. Turn the cakes out of their tins on to wire racks to cool while you make the frosting.

Put the sugar and water into a saucepan and heat gently until the sugar has dissolved completely, then boil until a teaspoon of the syrup, dropped into a mug of cold water, forms a soft ball.

Meanwhile, whisk the egg whites until they are stiff. When the syrup reaches the soft ball stage, add the vanilla essence and pour in a steady stream on to the stiff egg whites, whisking continuously as you pour. Whisk until the mixture is very thick.

Put one chocolate cake on a serving plate and spread some of the thick white frosting over it. Put the remaining cake on top and cover the whole cake, top and sides, with the remaining thick white frosting. Leave the cake in a cool place to set.

HAZELNUT AND APPLE CHOCOLATE CAKE

This is a very moist apple and hazelnut cake, with a covering of chocolate buttercream.

SERVES 6-8

For the cake
450g (1 lb) dessert apples
175 (6oz) soft light brown sugar
150ml (¼ pint) sunflower oil
3 large eggs
175g (6oz) self-raising flour
5ml (1 tsp) bicarbonate of soda
75g (3oz) hazelnuts, whizzed in a blender or processor to large crumb size, then toasted until pale golden, and cooled
10ml (2 tsp) ground cinnamon

For the buttercream
225g (8oz) butter
225g (8oz) icing sugar
100g (4oz) dark chocolate
2.5ml (½ tsp) vanilla essence
75g (3oz) dark chocolate curls (see page 94)

To make the apple pureé, chop but do not peel or core the apples and cook in a very little water until soft. Rub through a sieve and leave to cool.

Butter two 22.5 cm (9 inch) sandwich cake tins, and line the base of each with non-stick baking parchment.

Mix together the apple pureé and the sugar, then stir in the oil. Beat in the eggs, one at a time. Stir in the flour sieved with the soda, the hazelnuts and cinnamon. Mix all together well.

Divide the mixture between the two prepared tins, smooth the tops and bake in the oven preheated to 180°C (350°F/Gas Mark 4), or the bottom right oven in a four-door Aga, for 25–30 minutes, until a skewer stuck in the centre of the cakes comes out clean. Remove the cakes from the oven and leave to cool in their tins for 5 minutes, then turn them on to wire racks and leave to cool completely. Peel off the lining paper.

To make the buttercream, cream the butter, gradually adding the icing sugar, and beat until the mixture is fluffy. Break the chocolate into a small bowl and aldd 15 ml (1 tbsp) water. Stand the bowl over a pan of simmering water and heat gently, stirring occasionally, until the chocolate is melted. Cool slightly, then beat into the buttercream.

Put one of the cakes on a serving plate and spread with some of the buttercream. Put the remaining cake on top and cover the top and sides of the cake with the rest of the buttercream. Sprinkle with the chocolate curls. Leave the cake in a cool place until set.

Devil's Food Cake with American Frosting (page 40)

Hazelnut and Apple Chocolate Cake (page 41)

CHESTNUT AND CHOCOLATE CREAM SPONGE CAKE

This is a soft chocolate sponge cake with a rich filling of chocolate-flavoured sweetened chestnut pureé folded into whipped cream. The same chestnut mixture covers the top and sides of the cake, which is decorated by strips of paper being laid diagonally across the top, and icing sugar mixed with cocoa sieved over the surface. When the strips of paper are removed, the cake has a diagonally striped effect. This cake, like all sponge cakes, is most easily cut into slices with a serrated knife.

SERVES 8
For the cake
4 large eggs
100g (4oz) caster sugar
75g (3oz) self-raising flour
25g (1oz) cocoa powder

For the chestnut and chocolate cream
425g (15oz) can sweetened chestnut pureé
175g (6oz) dark chocolate, melted
300ml (½ pint) double cream

For the decoration
25g (1oz) icing sugar
15g (½ oz) cocoa powder

Butter two 22.5cm (9 inch) sandwich cake tins and line the base of each with a disc of non-stick baking parchment. To make the cake, whisk the eggs in a bowl, gradually adding the sugar. Whisk continuously until the mixture is so thick that a trail from the end of the whisk holds its shape on the surface of the mixture – about 10 minutes, using a hand-held electric whisk.

Sieve together the flour and cocoa powder and sieve again into the bowl. Using a large metal spoon, fold the flour and cocoa powder quickly and thoroughly through the mixture, taking care not to leave any pockets of flour. Divide the mixture between the prepared tins and smooth the tops. Bake in the oven pre-heated to 180°C (350°F/Gas Mark 4), or the bottom right oven in a four-door Aga, for 20 minutes, or until the sides of the cakes are just beginning to shrink away from the sides of the tins. Remove the cakes from the oven, leave to cool for 2 minutes in the tins, then turn them on to wire racks and leave to cool completely. When cold, peel off lining paper.

To make the chestnut and chocolate cream, put the chestnut pureé into a blender or food processor and whizz until smooth. Add the melted chocolate and whizz again until well mixed. Carefully fold together the chestnut and chocolate mixture and the cream, whipped until it just holds its shape.

To assemble the cake, slice each cake in half horizontally. Put one of the cakes on a serving plate, spread with some of the chestnut and chocolate cream, then put a second cake on top.

Repeat with the remaining cakes. Spread the remaining chestnut and chocolate cream over the top and sides of the cake.

Cut five strips of greaseproof paper about 1 cm (½ inch) wide, and lay them evenly and diagonally across the cake. About 2 hours (not much longer) before serving the cake, mix together the icing sugar and cocoa and sieve over the cake. Carefully lift off each paper strip, to leave a prettily striped effect. Cut with a serrated knife.

TOASTED COCONUT AND CHOCOLATE CREAM CAKE

This light, vanilla flavoured sponge cake is filled and covered with whipped cream and toasted coconut, with a layer of grated dark chocolate in the filling and on top of the cake. The combination of the flavours of toasted coconut and dark chocolate is sublime.

SERVES 8
For the cake
3 large eggs
75 g (3 oz) caster sugar
75 g (3 oz) self-raising flour
5 ml (1 tsp) vanilla essence

For the filling and covering
450 ml (¾ pint) double cream
100 g (4 oz) desiccated coconut, toasted until golden, then cooled completely
225 g (8 oz) dark chocolate, grated

*B*utter two 20 cm (8 inch) sandwich cake tins and line the base of each with a disc of non-stick baking parchment. To make the cake, whisk the eggs into a bowl, gradually adding the sugar. Continue whisking until the mixture is so thick that a trail from the end of the whisk holds its shape on the surface of the mixture. This takes about 7–10 minutes, using a hand-held electric whisk.

Sieve the flour and fold it and the vanilla essence thoroughly through the egg mixture, using a large metal spoon. Divide the mixture between the two prepared tins and smooth the tops. Bake in the oven pre-heated to 180°C (350°F/Gas Mark 4), or the bottom right oven in a four-door Aga, for 20–25 minutes, or until the sides of the cakes are just beginning to shrink away from the sides of the tins. Remove the cakes from the oven, leave to cool for a couple of minutes in their tins, then turn them on to wire racks and leave to cool completely. When they are cold, peel off the lining paper.

To make the coconut cream for the filling and covering, whip the cream fairly stiffly and fold in the coconut. To assemble the cake, put one of the cakes on a serving dish and spread with some of the coconut cream. Sprinkle over some of the grated chocolate. Put the remaining cake on top. Cover the top and sides of the cake with the remaining coconut cream. Sprinkle the remaining grated chocolate over the top of the cake. Keep the cake in a cool place until you are ready to serve it. Use a serrated knife to cut the cake.

Chestnut and Chocolate Cream Sponge Cake (page 44)

Toasted Coconut and Chocolate Cream Cake (page 45)

CHOCOLATE MOUSSE CAKE

This is a heavenly combination of rich, squidgy chocolate cake with a soft, creamy chocolate mousse on top. It is made in a springform tin, carefully unmoulded on to a serving plate, and served cut in wedges. If you like, you can decorate the surface of the mousse cake with piped rosettes of whipped cream, with a little grated chcolate sprinkled on each rosette, or you can leave the cake plain – it's perfectly delicious!

SERVES 8-10
For the cake
175g (6oz) dark chocolate
5 large eggs, separated
150g (5oz) caster sugar
30ml (2tbsp) orange liqueur, such as Cointreau

For the mousse
5ml (1tsp) powdered gelatine
juice of 1 orange
175g (6oz) dark chocolate
30ml (2tbsp) orange liqueur
4 eggs, separated
150ml (¼ pint) double cream

For the decoration (optional)
150ml (¼ pint) double cream, whipped
a little grated dark chocolate

*B*utter a 25cm (10inch) springform cake tin and line the base with a disc of non-stick baking parchment. To make the cake, break the chocolate into a heatproof bowl set over a saucepan of gently simmering water (take care not to let the bottom of the bowl touch the water). Heat gently until the chocolate has melted, then take the bowl off the heat.

In another bowl beat the egg yolks, gradually adding the caster sugar and the liqueur. Beat until the mixture is thick and pale. Stir in the cooled melted chocolate. Whisk the egg whites until they are stiff, and, using a large metal spoon, fold them quickly and thoroughly through the chocolate mixture. Pour this into the prepared tin and bake in the oven pre-heated to 180°C (350°F/Gas Mark 4), or the bottom right oven in a four-door Aga, for 35 minutes, until a skewer inserted into the centre of the cake comes out clean. Remove the cake from the oven and leave to cool in the tin (about 1 hour).

To make the mousse, sprinkle the gelatine over the orange juice in a small saucepan, then heat through very gently until the gelatine granules have dissolved completely. Break the chocolate into a heatproof bowl set over a saucepan of gently simmering water (take care not to let the bottom of the bowl touch the water). Heat gently until the chocolate has melted. Take the bowl off the heat and stir in the liqueur and the liquid gelatine.

Beat the egg yolks into the chocolate mixture, one by one, and leave them to cool for 5 minutes, then fold in the cream, whipped until it just holds its shape. Whisk the egg whites until they are very stiff, and, using a large metal spoon, fold them quickly and thoroughly into the chocolate mousse.

With your fingertips, press down the sugary crust on top of the cooled cake – this will have formed during baking. Pour the mousse on top of the cake in the tin and leave for several hours, or overnight, to set.

To serve, dip a palette knife in hot water and run it round the inside of the tin. Undo the spring sides of the tin, and, using a fish slice, carefully ease the cake on to a serving plate. Decorate, if you like, with rosettes of whipped cream piped around the edge of the top of the mousse, and a little grated chocolate sprinkled over the rosettes.

Nègre en Chemise

Really a stiff pudding rather than a true cake, this is really rich and delicious – very convenient, too, because I think it is actually nicer the day after it is made. It is simple to make, and the thick layer of whipped cream on top (the so-called 'chemise' in the name of the pud) can be added a few hours before the pudding is served.

SERVES 6-8
225 g (8 oz) ground almonds
225 g (8 oz) butter
225 g (8 oz) dark chocolate
4 large eggs, separated
225 g (8 oz) caster sugar
300 ml (½ pint) double cream

Toast the ground almonds until golden, then set aside to cool.

Put the butter and chocolate in a saucepan and heat gently until they have melted together. Remove the pan from the heat and stir. Leave to cool.

Whisk the egg yolks, gradually adding the sugar. Whisk really well until the mixture is pale and thick. Stir the cooled, melted chocolate and butter into the yolk mixture, then stir in the toasted ground almonds.

Whisk the egg whites until they are very stiff, and, using a large metal spoon, fold them quickly and thoroughly through the chocolate mixture which will be very stiff, but as you fold in the whisked whites the mixture slackens.

Pour into a glass serving bowl, and leave in a cool place. Several hours before serving, whip the cream until it is fairly stiff, then spread over the chocolate pudding.

CHOCOLATE PROFITEROLES WITH ORANGE CREAM AND CHOCOLATE SAUCE

For so many people this is a favourite way of eating a chocolate-based pudding. Sadly, a lot of people have hang-ups about making choux pastry – quite unnecessarily so because it really is very straightforward. Filled with an orange-flavoured whipped cream, these profiteroles are absolutely delicious and look stunning arranged in a pyramid to serve.

SERVES 6-8
For the choux pastry
150g (5oz) butter, diced
300ml (½ pint) water
200g (7oz) flour, sieved
4-5 large eggs

For the filling
450ml (¾ pint) double cream
50g (2oz) caster sugar
grated rind of 2 oranges
15ml (1 tbsp) orange liqueur

Add the butter to the water in a saucepan. Melt the butter in the water over a moderate heat and when it is completely melted, let the liquid come to the boil. Add the flour all at once, remove the pan from the heat and beat the mixture hard until it just begins to come away from the sides of the pan. Let it cool for a few minutes, then beat in the eggs, one by one, beating really hard so that you have a smooth, glossy paste.

Rinse two baking trays with water: the water on the baking trays evaporates into steam which helps the profiteroles to rise during baking. Pipe the choux pastry mixture, using a star nozzle, into even-sized blobs about the size of a 10p piece.

Bake in the oven, pre-heated to 200°C (400°F/Gas Mark 6), or the top right-hand oven in a four-door Aga, for 15–20 minutes, swapping the trays around halfway through cooking time. Cut a little slit in each profiterole and pop the baking trays back into the oven for a few minutes to let the steam evaporate from within each profiterole. Then remove from the oven and transfer them to a wire cooling rack to cool.

To make the filling, whip the cream until stiff, gradually adding the sugar. Fold in the orange rind and liqueur. Pipe into the profiteroles and serve with Dark Chocolate Sauce (page 92).

Chocolate Profiteroles with Orange Cream and Chocolate Sauce (page 50)

ROULADES

Roulades are wonderful, all so different with their various flavour combinations. Prune and Armagnac with cream, raspberries and cream, and a tangy apricot and lemon purée are just some of the fillings for the chocolate roulades in this section. They look good, they are easy to serve in thick slices; they are easy, too, to eat, so they make ideal puddings for buffet parties.

CHOCOLATE AND COFFEE ROULADE

This is such a good roulade, densely chocolatey with the flavour highlighted by the coffee.

SERVES 8
For the roulade
175 g (6 oz) dark chocolate
10 ml (2 tsp) instant coffee dissolved in 60 ml (4 tbsp) boiling water
6 large eggs, separated
175 g (6 oz) caster sugar

For the filling
450 ml (¾ pint) double cream
45 ml (3 tbsp) coffee liqueur such as Tia Maria or Kahlúa

Line a baking tray about 35 × 40 cm (14 × 16 inches) with non-stick baking parchment. To make the roulade, break the chocolate into a heatproof bowl and add the coffee liquid. Put the bowl over a saucepan of gently simmering water (take care not to let the bottom of the bowl touch the water). Heat gently until the chocolate has melted, then take the bowl off the heat. Stir just until mixed.

Meanwhile, whisk the egg yolks in a bowl, gradually adding the sugar, and whisk until the mixture is very pale and thick. Stir in the chocolate and coffee mixture.

Whisk the egg whites until they are very stiff, and, using a large metal spoon, carefully and thoroughly fold the whites through the chocolate mixture. Pour on to the prepared baking tray and spread out evenly. Bake in the oven pre-heated to 180°C (350°F/Gas Mark 4), or the bottom right oven in a four-door Aga, for 20–25 minutes or until the mixture springs back when pressed lightly with a finger. Remove the roulade from the oven, cover with a damp tea-towel and leave for several hours, or overnight.

Put a sheet of non-stick baking parchment on a work surface and sieve a spoonful of icing sugar over it. Take the tea-towel off the roulade, and taking the shorter ends of the paper under the roulade in either hand, tip it face down onto the icing sugar. Carefully peel off the lining paper, tearing the paper in strips horizontal to the roulade – that way you won't tear it.

Whip the cream for the filling with the liqueur, until it just holds its shape. Spread the liqueur-flavoured whipped cream over the surface of the roulade, taking it right to the edges. Roll up lengthways, then slip the roulade on to a serving plate or tray. (You can do this in the morning for dinner that night). Dust with icing sugar and serve in slices about 4 cm (1½ inches) thick.

CHOCOLATE ROULADE WITH PRUNE AND ARMAGNAC CREAM

This unusual roulade has a luxurious filling of cream well-flavoured with Armagnac, and containing chopped prunes.

SERVES 8
For the roulade
175 g (6 oz) dark chocolate
6 large eggs, separated
175 g (6 oz) caster sugar
sieved icing sugar, to finish

For the filling
300 ml (½ pint) double cream
60 ml (4 tbsp) Armagnac
8–10 large prunes, soaked, simmered until plump in china tea, then well-drained, stoned and chopped

Line a baking tray about 35 × 40 cm (14 × 16 inches) with non-stick baking parchment. To make the roulade, break the chocolate into a heatproof bowl, set over a saucepan of gently simmering water (take care not to let the bottom of the bowl touch the water). Heat gently until the chocolate has melted, then take the bowl off the heat.

Meanwhile, whisk the egg yolks in a bowl, gradually adding the caster sugar. Whisk until the mixture is very pale and very thick. Stir in the melted chocolate. Whisk the egg whites until they are very stiff, and, using a large metal spoon, fold them quickly and thoroughly through the chocolate mixture. Pour on to the prepared baking tray and bake in the oven pre-heated to 180°C (350°F/Gas Mark 4), or the bottom right oven in a four-door Aga, for 20–25 minutes or until the mixture springs back when pressed lightly with a finger. Remove from the oven and cover with a damp tea-towel. Leave until quite cold.

To make the filling, whip the cream until it just holds its shape and whip in the Armagnac and fold in the chopped prunes. Put a sheet of non-stick baking parchment on a work surface and dust with a spoonful of sieved icing sugar. Remove the tea-towel from the roulade and tip it face down on the icing sugar. Carefully peel off the paper lining, tearing it in strips horizontal to the roulade to avoid tearing it. Spread the prune and Armagnac cream over the roulade and roll up lengthways. Dust with more icing sugar before serving.

Chocolate and Coffee Roulade (page 52)

Orange and Lemon Roulade with Chocolate Cream (page 56)

ORANGE AND LEMON ROULADE WITH CHOCOLATE CREAM

This roulade has a soft orange and lemon flavoured sponge base rolled up around whipped cream containing grated dark chocolate.

SERVES 8
For the roulade
5 large eggs, separated
150 g (5 oz) caster sugar
grated rind and juice of 1 lemon
grated rind of 1 orange
50 g (2 oz) ground almonds
icing sugar for dusting

For the filling
300 ml (½ pint) double cream
45 ml (3 tbsp) orange liqueur (optional)
100 g (4 oz) dark chocolate, coarsely grated

Line a baking tray about 35 × 40 cm (14 × 16 inches) with non-stick baking parchment. To make the roulade, whisk the egg yolks in a bowl, gradually adding the caster sugar and whisking until the mixture is pale and very thick. Whisk in the lemon juice, and fold in the sieved ground almonds and the grated lemon and orange rinds. Whisk the egg whites until they are very stiff, then, using a large metal spoon, fold them quickly and thoroughly through the lemon and orange mixture. Pour this on to the prepared baking tray.

Bake in the oven pre-heated to 180°C (350°F/Gas Mark 4), or the bottom right oven in a four-door Aga, for 20–25 minutes or until the mixture springs back when pressed lightly with a finger. Remove the roulade from the oven and cover with a damp tea-towel. Leave for several hours or overnight.

To make the filling, whip the cream with the liqueur if used, until it just holds its shape and fold in the grated chocolate. Take care not to whip the cream until too stiff, otherwise the filling will be very stiff once the grated chocolate is folded in.

Put a sheet of non-stick baking parchment on a work surface and sieve a spoonful of icing sugar over it. Remove the tea-towel from the roulade and tip it face down on the icing sugar. Carefully peel off the lining paper, tearing it off in strips horizontal to the roulade, to prevent tearing it.

Spread the roulade with the grated chocolate and whipped cream mixture, spreading it out as evenly as possible with a spatula. Roll up the roulade lengthways and slip it on to a serving plate or tray. Dust with more icing sugar, if you like, before serving.

CHOCOLATE CRISP ROULADE WITH RASPBERRIES AND CREAM

A thin coating of melted chocolate spread over the surface of the cooked roulade before the raspberries and cream are spread on helps to prevent the base from being made soggy by the filling, although the roulade does crack at the sides as it is rolled up. However, a good dusting of sieved icing sugar hides a multitude of cracks!

SERVES 8
For the roulade
175 g (6 oz) dark chocolate
6 large eggs, separated
175 g (6 oz) caster sugar
mint sprigs, to decorate

For the filling
75 g (3 oz) dark chocolate
45 ml (¾ pint) double cream
25 g (1 oz) caster sugar
225 g (8 oz) fresh raspberries, or thawed and well-drained frozen raspberries
icing sugar

Line a 30 × 35 cm (12 × 14 inch) baking tray or Swiss roll tin with non-stick baking parchment.

To make the roulade, break the chocolate into a heatproof bowl, set over a saucepan of gently simmering water (take care not to let the bottom of the bowl touch the water). Heat gently until melted.

Whisk the egg yolks with the caster sugar until thick and pale, then beat in the cooled melted chocolate. Whisk the egg whites until they are very stiff, and, using a large metal spoon, fold them quickly and thoroughly through the chocolate mixture. Pour this on to the prepared baking tray and spread out evenly. Bake in the oven preheated to 180°C (350°F/Gas Mark 4), or the bottom right oven in a four-door Aga, for 20–25 minutes or until the mixture springs back when pressed lightly with a finger. Remove from oven and cover with a damp tea-towel until cold.

To make the filling, break the chocolate into a heatproof bowl and melt over a pan of hot water. Whip the cream with the sugar until it just holds its shape. Reserve a third of it for the top, then mix the remainder with most of the raspberries.

Put a sheet of non-stick baking parchment on a table or work surface, dust it with sieved icing sugar and turn the cooled roulade on to it. Carefully peel off the lining paper, tearing it into strips horizontal to the roulade – this way, it won't tear with the paper. Using a palette knife, spread the hot melted chocolate over the surface of the roulade, and leave to cool.

Spread the cream and raspberry mixture evenly over the roulade and roll it up lengthways. Dust with more icing sugar, pipe the reserved cream along the top and decorate with raspberries and mint sprigs.

CHOCOLATE AND APRICOT ROULADE

This roulade is delicious and also very good for those who like to cut down on their intake of cream, because the filling is a lemon-flavoured purée of dried apricots, lightened with egg yolks.

SERVES 8
For the roulade
175g (6oz) dark chocolate
6 large eggs, separated
175g (6oz) caster sugar
sieved icing sugar, to finish

For the filling
350g (12oz) dried apricots
thinly pared rind of 1 lemon
2 large egg yolks
50g (5oz) caster sugar

*F*irst make the filling. Put the apricots into a saucepan with the lemon rind and water to cover. Simmer gently for 40 minutes or until the apricots are tender and well plumped up. Drain very well, then put the drained apricots and lemon rind into a blender or food processor. Whizz until they are a smooth purée, adding the egg yolks, one at a time, and the caster sugar. Whizz until paler in colour – about 5 minutes – then let this mixture cool while you make the roulade.

Break the chocolate into a heatproof bowl, set over a saucepan of gently simmering water (take care not to let the bottom of the bowl touch the water). Heat gently until the chocolate has melted, then take the bowl off the heat.

Whisk the egg yolks in a bowl, gradually adding the sugar, and whisk until the mixture is very pale and very thick. Stir in the melted chocolate.

Line a baking tray measuring about 35 × 40 cm (14 × 16 inches) with non-stick baking parchment. Whisk the egg whites until they are very stiff, then, using a large metal spoon, fold them quickly and thoroughly through the chocolate mixture. Pour on to the prepared baking tray, and spread out evenly. Bake in the oven pre-heated to 180°C (350°F/Gas Mark 4), or the bottom right oven in a four-door Aga, for 20–25 minutes or until firm. Remove the roulade from the oven, cover with a damp tea-towel and leave for several hours or overnight.

Put a sheet of non-stick baking parchment on a work surface and dust a spoonful of sieved icing sugar over it. Take the tea-towel off the baked roulade, and tip it face down on to the icing sugar. Tear off the parchment in horizontal strips – that way you won't tear the roulade itself. Spread the apricot filling mixture evenly over the surface and roll up the sponge lengthways. Slip the roulade on to a serving dish or tray and dust with more sieved icing sugar before serving.

Chocolate Velvet Cream Pie (page 60)

CREAM PIES AND CHEESECAKES

There is something mouth-watering about chocolate pies – I think it is the combination of crisp, vanilla-flavoured pastry with the smooth creamy chocolate fillings which appeals to me, and, judging how popular chocolate pies are when they feature on the menu here at Kinloch, to a lot of other people too. All the pies in the chapter are convenient in that they don't involve any last-minute preparation or finishing off.

In this chapter you will also find two ideas for chocolate cheesecakes, both completely different, and each quite delicious.

CHOCOLATE VELVET CREAM PIE

This pie has a base not of pastry but of crushed chocolate digestive biscuits mixed with melted butter. The filling contains cream cheese, and is smooth and silky in texture.

SERVES 6-8
For the base
250 g (9 oz) packet dark chocolate digestive biscuits
75 g (3 oz) butter, melted and cooled

For the filling
225 g (8 oz) cream cheese
175 g (6 oz) caster sugar
5 ml (1 tsp) vanilla essence
175 g (6 oz) dark chocolate, melted
2 large egg yolks
300 ml (½ pint) double cream
1 large egg white
50 g (2 oz) caster sugar

To make the base, crush the biscuits to crumbs in a blender or food processor, or in a polythene bag with a rolling pin. Mix together the biscuit crumbs and the cooled melted butter, and press round the base and sides of a 20–22.5 cm (8–9 inch) flan dish. Bake in the oven pre-heated to 180°C (350°F/Gas Mark 4), or the bottom right oven in a four-door Aga, for 15 minutes. Remove and leave to cool.

To make the filling, beat together the cream cheese and 100 g (4 oz) of the caster sugar. Beat in the vanilla essence and the melted chocolate, and the egg yolks, one by one. Fold in the cream, whipped until it just holds its shape. Whisk the egg whites until they are stiff, then, still whisking, add the remaining caster sugar a spoonful at a time. Fold into the chocolate mixture. Pour the mixture into the cooled baked pie crust. Chill in the fridge for several hours until set.

HOT BAKED CHOCOLATE CHEESECAKE

You can eat this cheesecake cold, but it is much nicer hot – it keeps warm very satisfactorily for 20 minutes or so in a low oven.

SERVES 6
For the base
100 g (4 oz) chilled butter
150 g (5 oz) flour
25 g (1 oz) icing sugar
a few drops of vanilla essence

For the filling
225 g (8 oz) cream cheese
225 g (8 oz) soft light brown sugar
a few drops of vanilla essence
50 g (2 oz) cocoa
4 large eggs
sieved icing sugar, to finish

To make the base, whizz all the ingredients for the base together in a food processor until the mixture resembles breadcrumbs. Alternatively, cut the butter into the flour and icing sugar with a knife, then rub in with your fingertips until it reaches the breadcrumb stage. Press this mixture round the base of a 20–22.5 cm (8–9 inch) flan dish. Chill the flan in the fridge for 30 minutes then bake in the oven pre-heated to 180°C (350°F/Gas Mark 4), or the bottom right oven of a four-door Aga, for 25–30 minutes, until the pastry is pale golden brown. Remove from the oven, and leave to cool while you make the filling.

Put the cream cheese into a blender or food processor and whizz, gradually adding the sugar, then the vanilla essence, cocoa, 2 whole eggs and 2 egg yolks. Blend until smooth. Alternatively, mix all the ingredients very thoroughly in a bowl.

Whisk the remaining 2 egg whites until they are stiff, and, using a large metal spoon, fold them quickly and thoroughly through the chocolate mixture. Pour into the cooked pastry shell, and bake in the oven pre-heated to 180°C (350°F/Gas Mark 4), or the bottom right oven of a four-door Aga, for 35–40 minutes, until set. Dust with icing sugar to serve.

Hot Baked Chocolate Cheesecake, Dark Chocolate-Dipped Strawberries (pages 61 and 89)

Chocolate Pecan Pie (page 64)

CHOCOLATE PECAN PIE

This yummy pie has a hint of coffee in the flavouring, which combines so well with the chocolate and the pecans. Pecans are widely available now in good grocers' shops and delicatessens. They are not always in the freshest condition, though, and I always put them in a saucepan over a moderate heat, shaking them from time to time to prevent them from burning, for 5–7 minutes, then cool them, and this freshens them up. If you can't find pecans, substitute walnuts and give them the same freshening-up treatment.

SERVES 6-8

For the pastry
100g (4oz) chilled butter
150g (5oz) flour
25g (1oz) icing sugar
a few drops of vanilla essence

For the filling
100g (4oz) butter, diced
100g (4oz) soft light brown sugar
50g (2oz) dark chocolate
5ml (1 tsp) instant coffee
3 large eggs, beaten
175g (6oz) shelled pecans

To make the pastry, cut the butter into bits in a food processor and add the flour, icing sugar and vanilla. Whizz for a few seconds, until the mixture resembles breadcrumbs. Or grate the butter into the sieved flour, rub in with the fingertips until the mixture resembles breadcrumbs, then stir in the icing sugar and vanilla essence. Knead lightly together, then press the mixture round the base and sides of a 22.5 cm (9 inch) flan dish. Chill in the fridge for at least 30 minutes, then bake in the oven pre-heated to 180°C (350°F/Gas Mark 4), or the bottom right oven in a four-door Aga. Bake for 20–25 minutes, until the pastry is golden. Remove from the oven and leave to cool.

To make the filling, put the butter into a heat-proof bowl with the sugar, chocolate and coffee granules. Set the bowl over a saucepan of gently simmering water until the butter has melted and the sugar dissolved.

When the butter mixture has melted remove the bowl from the heat and stir in the beaten eggs. Strew the pecans over the cooled baked pie crust, then pour in the chocolate mixture. Put the pie carefully (so as not to spill the filling) into the oven pre-heated to 180°C (350°F/Gas Mark 4), or the bottom right oven of a four-door Aga, for 20–25 minutes, until the filling is just firm to the touch.

I like to serve this pie warm with whipped cream – it is nicest eaten soon after it is baked, rather than being made and reheated.

CHOCOLATE AND GINGER CREAM PIE

I love ginger and chocolate: in this pie, the pastry has ground ginger in it, there is ginger wine in the filling, and slivers of preserved ginger round the top of the chocolate filling.

SERVES 6-8
For the pastry
100g (4oz) chilled butter
150g (5oz) flour
25g (1oz) icing sugar
10ml (2tsp) ground ginger

For the filling
100g (4oz) dark chocolate
300ml (½ pint) milk
5ml (1tsp) powdered gelatine
60ml (4tbsp) ginger wine
3 large eggs, separated
5ml (1tsp) cornflour
75g (3oz) caster sugar
300ml (½ pint) double cream
8 pieces of ginger, drained and cut into slivers
chocolate squares (see page 94)

To make the pastry, cut the butter into bits in a food processor and add the flour, icing sugar and ginger. Whizz until the mixture resembles breadcrumbs. Or grate the butter into the sieved flour, rub in with the fingertips until the mixture resembles breadcrumbs, then stir in the sieved icing sugar and ginger. Press the mixture around the base and sides of a 20–22.5 cm (8–9 inch) flan dish. Chill in the fridge for at least 30 minutes, then bake in the oven pre-heated to 180°C (350°F/Gas Mark 4), or the bottom right oven in a four-door Aga, for 20–25 minutes, until the pastry is golden. Remove and leave to cool.

To make the filling, break the chocolate into the milk in a saucepan, and heat gently until melted. Sprinkle the gelatine over the ginger wine in a small saucepan and heat very gently until the gelatine granules have dissolved completely – do not let it boil. Whisk together the egg yolks, sugar and cornflour until well blended, then pour on to them a little of the hot chocolate milk. Mix well, then pour back into the saucepan containing the remaining chocolate and milk. Stir over a moderate heat until the mixture coats the back of the spoon thickly enough to leave a distinct 'path' when you draw your finger down the middle. Take it off the heat, stir in the ginger wine and gelatine, and leave to cool completely, giving an occasional stir to prevent a skin from forming.

When the mixture is quite cold, fold in the cream, whipped until it just holds its shape. Whisk two of the egg whites, until they are very stiff (keep the remaining egg white for meringues) and, using a large metal spoon, fold them quickly and thoroughly through the chocolate cream. Pour into the cooled pastry crust. Leave in a cool place for several hours to set before arranging the slivers of preserved ginger and the chocolate squares round the edges of the pie.

Chocolate and Ginger Cream Pie (page 65)

Chocolate Banana Cheesecake (page 68)

CHOCOLATE BANANA CHEESECAKE

If you have a food processor, this cheesecake doesn't take a minute to make, and it only takes a bit longer if you don't – yet! – have a food processor.

SERVES 6-8

For the base
12 dark chocolate digestive biscuits
75 g (3 oz) butter, melted
50 g (2 oz) demerara sugar

For the filling
4 bananas
225 g (8 oz) cream cheese
100 g (4 oz) soft light or dark brown sugar
4 large eggs
5 ml (1 tsp) vanilla essence

For the topping
300 ml (½ pint) double cream
2 bananas, peeled and thinly sliced
50 g (2 oz) dark chocolate, coarsely grated

To make the base, crush the biscuits to crumbs in a blender or food processor, or in a polythene bag with a rolling pin. Mix well with the butter and sugar. Press the mixture round the base of a 20–22.5 cm (8–9 inch) flan dish. Bake in the oven pre-heated to 180°C (350°F/Gas Mark 4), or the bottom right oven in a four-door Aga, for 15 minutes. Remove from the oven and leave to cool completely while you make the filling.

Purée the bananas in a food processor or mash them in a bowl with a fork to get as smooth a purée as you can. Add the cream cheese and mix with the bananas until smooth. Add the sugar, the eggs one at a time, and the vanilla essence and whizz until the mixture is smooth, or use an electric whisk to get as smooth a mixture as possible.

Pour the filling into the cooled cheesecake base and bake in the oven pre-heated to 180°C (350°F/Gas Mark 4), or the bottom right oven in a four-door Aga, for 35–40 minutes, until firm to the touch. Remove the cheesecake from the oven and allow to cool completely. Then spread the surface with cream, whipped until fairly stiff, arrange the banana slices around the edge at the last minute to avoid discolouring. Sprinkle evenly with the grated chocolate.

You can make and bake the base a day in advance, and make the cheesecake in the morning for serving at dinner that evening.

FAMILY FAVOURITES

These are supposedly meant for children, but in my experience they are every bit as popular with the more grown-up members of the family! In this chapter there are recipes which are perfect for family lunch parties, such as Baked Spiced Chocolate Meringue Pudding (page 76), and Pears with Hot Chocolate Sauce (page 76), and the pancake recipes (page 72 and 79). More homely puddings include Chocolate and Vanilla Cornflour Pudding: one of the earliest things I remember about my grandmother is eating this pudding with her. Baked Chocolate Pudding (page 77), called 'Chocolate Mud' by our children, and Chocolate Fudge Brownies (page 72), both served with Vanilla Iced Cream (page 29) as an embellishment, are two of our children's favourites.

PETITS POTS AU CHOCOLAT

These pots of chocolate are a classic French favourite. I've added a hint of coffee to the chocolate cream. One pot per person is quite enough; they're small but very rich.

SERVES 8
15 ml (1 level tbsp) coffee beans
3 large egg yolks
1 large egg
75 g (3 oz) caster sugar
900 ml (1 ½ pints) milk
75 g (3 oz) dark chocolate, broken up
150 ml (¼ pint) whipping cream
chocolate triangles (see page 94)

Toast the coffee beans under a moderate grill for a few minutes, then set aside.

Beat together the egg yolks, egg and sugar until the mixture is very pale. Put the milk and coffee beans into a saucepan and bring to the boil. Strain the hot milk on to the egg mixture, stirring all the time. Discard the coffee beans. Return the mixture to the saucepan, then add the chocolate. Stir over a gentle heat (do not boil) for about 5 minutes until the chocolate has almost melted and the mixture is *slightly* thickened.

Pour into individual 150 ml (¼ pint) ramekin dishes or custard pots. Put in a roasting tin, then pour in enough hot water to come halfway up the sides of the dishes. Bake at 150°C (300°F/Gas Mark 2), or in the bottom right oven in a four-door Aga, for 1–2 hours or until lightly set.

Leave to cool. To serve, decorate the pots with piped cream and chocolate triangles.

Petits Pots au Chocolat (page 69)

Chocolate Fudge Brownies (page 72)

CHOCOLATE FUDGE BROWNIES

It is vital that these yummy brownies be served with Vanilla Iced Cream (page 29). They are very chocolatey and very good. They actually keep quite well in a tin, but the opportunity does not usually arise, because people don't stop eating them! They need to be under-cooked, so test by sticking a knife or skewer in the middle and it should come out still with mixture clinging to it. If you don't like walnuts, just leave them out of the recipe. And do try making them with pecans instead of walnuts – they are even more delicious then!

MAKES ABOUT 16
100 g (4 oz) butter, diced
100 g (4 oz) dark chocolate
300 g (10 oz) soft light brown sugar
4 large eggs, beaten
225 g (8 oz) self-raising flour
40 g (1 ½ oz) cocoa powder
75 g (3 oz) walnuts, chopped

*B*utter and flour (or line with non-stick baking parchment) a baking tin about 30 x 35 cm (12 x 14 inches).

Put the butter and chocolate, broken into bits, into a saucepan and melt together over a gentle heat. Add all the remaining ingredients and mix together very well. Pour this mixture into the pre-pared tin and bake in the oven pre-heated to 180°C (350°F/Gas Mark 4), or the bottom right oven of a four-door Aga, for about 15 minutes, until still sticky in the middle. Remove from the oven and cool in the tin. When cold, cut into small squares or rectangles and store in an airtight container. Serve warm, with Vanilla Iced Cream (page 29).

CINNAMON PANCAKES WITH CHOCOLATE CREAM

The pancakes can be made up a day or two in advance and kept in the refrigerator in a sealed polythene bag, with a disc of non-stick parch-ment between each pancake. Fill and roll them up several hours before serving.

SERVES 8
For the batter
150 g (5 oz) flour
10 ml (2 tsp) ground cinnamon
25 g (1 oz) caster sugar
25 g (1 oz) butter, melted
2 large eggs
300 ml (½ pint) milk
150 ml (¼ pint) water

For the filling
300 ml (½ pint) double cream
100 g (4 oz) dark chocolate, grated

To finish
15 ml (1 tbsp) icing sugar, sieved

irst make the batter. In a blender or food processor, whizz together all the batter ingredients until smooth. Let the mixture stand for about 1 hour, then make into pancakes, as thin as possible.

To make the pancakes (it is so much easier and quicker if you happen to have two crêpe pans which you can use simultaneously), put a small piece of butter – about 15 ml (½ oz) – into the pan, and melt over a fairly high heat. Pour in a small amount of batter, swirling it round so that it coats the base of the pan as thinly as possible. After a minute or so, turn the pancake over with the help of a small palette knife (and your fingers!). Let it cook for about a minute on the other side. As they cook, stack the pancakes on a plate or cooling rack. (I put a piece of non-stick bakewell or greaseproof paper between each pancake.)

To make the filling, fold together the cream, whipped until it holds its shape, and the chocolate. Divide the chocolate cream among the pancakes, allowing 2 pancakes per person. Fold the pancakes into rectangular parcels, tucking the ends under. Put them into a wide ovenproof dish.

Just before serving, heat the grill until it is red-hot. Dust the top of the pancakes with the icing sugar and pop the dish under the grill for just long enough to caramelize the sugar – count to 30! – and serve.

STEAMED CHOCOLATE PUDDING

This is a simple pud to make and such a good one to eat. If you have one of those heatproof plastic pudding bowls with a snap-on lid it makes the whole thing even simpler.

SERVES 6
75 g (3 oz) butter
100 g (4 oz) soft light brown sugar
2 large egg yolks
2.5 ml (½ tsp) vanilla essence
100 g (4 oz) dark chocolate
150 ml (¼ pint) milk
175 g (6 oz) fresh white breadcrumbs

utter a 900 ml (2 pint) pudding basin. Cream the butter with the sugar until fluffy. Beat in the egg yolks and the vanilla essence.

Break up the chocolate and melt it in the milk over a gentle heat. Cool slightly, then mix in the yolk and butter mixture, alternately with the breadcrumbs, until thoroughly combined. Lastly, whisk the egg whites until they are frothy, and, using a metal spoon, fold them thoroughly into the mixture.

Pour into the prepared bowl, cover with a disc of greaseproof paper, snap on the lid or tie on a cloth, and steam the pudding in a covered saucepan for 1 hour. Unmould to serve.

This pudding is delicious served with Vanilla Cream Sauce (page 91).

DARK CHOCOLATE RICE PUDDING

I do love rice pudding – proper rice pudding, that is, by which I mean baked rice pud. I know that some people cook rice pudding in a saucepan on top of the stove, but to me this isn't the right way to make it, because no delicious skin forms as it does when baked. This version of rice pudding, well flavoured with dark chocolate and vanilla, is really almost worthy of a dinner party, it is so good.

SERVES 6
900 ml (1½ pints) milk
100 g (4 oz) dark chocolate
50 g (2 oz) short-grain pudding rice
75 g (2 oz) caster sugar
2.5 ml (½ tsp) vanilla essence
50 g (2 oz) butter

*B*utter an ovenproof pudding dish or a soufflé dish.

Put the milk into a saucepan and break in the chocolate. Heat gently until the chocolate has melted. Stir in the rice, sugar and vanilla essence. Pour the mixture into the prepared dish and dot the surface with the butter. Bake in the oven preheated to 150°C (300°F/Gas Mark 2), or the bottom right oven in a four-door Aga, for 2 hours. Serve with cream.

CHOCOLATE AND VANILLA CORNFLOUR PUDDING

This is a nostalgic pudding for me, reminding me as it does of my grandmother, who obviously had the same craving for chocolate as I do!

SERVES 6
25 g (1 oz) cocoa powder
30 ml (2 tbsp) cornflour
75 g (3 oz) caster sugar
900 ml (1½ pints) milk
5 ml (1 tbsp) vanilla essence

*M*ix together the cocoa, cornflour and all but 15 ml (1 tbsp) of the sugar. Add a little of the milk and mix well to form a smooth paste. Stir in the vanilla essence.

Pour the remaining milk into a saucepan and heat it to just below boiling point, then pour some of the hot milk on to the chocolate and cornflour mixture. Mix well and pour it back into the saucepan containing the remaining milk. Over a moderate heat, stirring all the time, cook until the mixture bubbles. Pour into a soufflé or ovenproof pudding dish and sprinkle the remaining sugar over the surface, which helps to prevent a thick skin from forming. Serve warm, with cream.

Dark Chocolate Rice Pudding (page 74)

BAKED SPICED CHOCOLATE MERINGUE PUDDING

This is a lovely pudding. The chocolate part of it can be made up to a day in advance, but once the meringue has been baked on top it must be eaten soon.

SERVES 6
For the pudding base
600 ml (1 pint) hot milk
75 g (3 oz) dark chocolate
100 g (4 oz) soft light brown sugar
5 ml (1 tsp) ground cinnamon
a pinch of ground cloves
40 g (1½ oz) fresh white breadcrumbs, preferably from a baked, not steamed, loaf
25 g (1 oz) butter, diced
3 large egg yolks

For the meringue
3 large egg whites
175 g (6 oz) caster sugar

To make the base, put the milk in a saucepan with the broken-up chocolate and heat very gently until melted.

Mix together the sugar, cinnamon, cloves and breadcrumbs, and mix in the hot chocolate milk. Mix in the butter, stirring until melted, and beat in the egg yolks. Pour into a buttered pudding or soufflé dish and bake in the oven, pre-heated to 170°C (325°F/Gas Mark 3), or the bottom right oven in a four-door Aga, for 45 minutes, until firm to the touch.

For the meringue, whisk the egg whites until they are stiff, then, still whisking, add the sugar a spoonful at a time, until it is all incorporated and you have a stiff, glossy meringue. Pile the meringue on top of the baked chocolate pudding, smooth it out lightly, and return to the oven for 15 minutes, until crisp and pale golden. Serve immediately.

PEARS WITH HOT CHOCOLATE SAUCE

Although the recipe for this sauce is also given in the chapter on sauces, I am giving it to you again with this recipe, so that you will find it more convenient to follow. This simple pudding is exceptionally delicious. I like it best of all made with Comice pears, but you can of course make it with any pears. Ripe pears don't need any poaching — there are a surprising number of people who seem to think that if pears are served with a sauce they must first be cooked, but they are much nicer, if they are really ripe, simply peeled and cored, and covered with the sauce, as in this dish, which is very good served with Vanilla Iced Cream (page 29).

SERVES 6
6 ripe Comice or other pears

For the chocolate sauce
175 g (6 oz) caster or soft light brown sugar
90 ml (6 tbsp) cocoa powder
25 g (1 oz) butter
45 ml (3 tbsp) golden syrup (dip the spoon in boiling
water first, so that the syrup slips easily off the
spoon)
5 ml (1 tsp) vanilla essence
200 ml (7 fl oz) boiling water

*F*irst make the sauce. Put all the sauce ingredients into a saucepan and stir over a moderate heat until the sugar has dissolved completely. Then boil the sauce fast for 3–5 minutes.

Peel, quarter and core the pears. Cut each quarter in half lengthways. Put the pear segments into a shallow serving dish and pour the hot chocolate sauce over them.

If you want to make this dish ahead, allow the chocolate sauce to cool before pouring over the pears and pop the dish into a warm oven for 20 minutes to heat up before serving.

BAKED CHOCOLATE PUDDING

This pudding separates in cooking, to form a sponge-like top with a thick sauce underneath. It is quite delicious, especially so when served with Vanilla Iced Cream (page 29). For some reason this pud is referred to by our children as Chocolate Mud Pudding – not a very appealing name, but when mentioned it brings dreamy looks of yearning to their eyes!

SERVES 6
For the sponge
75 g (3 oz) soft light brown sugar
25 g (1 oz) cocoa powder
75 g (3 oz) self-raising flour, sieved
50 g (2 oz) butter, melted
3 large eggs, beaten
5 ml (1 tsp) vanilla essence

For the sauce
25 g (1 oz) cocoa powder
100 g (4 oz) soft light brown sugar

*T*o make the sponge, mix together the sugar, cocoa and flour. Stir in the melted butter, beaten eggs and vanilla essence and mix well together. Pour into a buttered ovenproof pudding dish or soufflé dish.

For the sauce, mix well together the cocoa, sugar and 450 ml (¾ pint) warm water and pour this on top of the pudding mixture in the dish. Bake in the oven pre-heated to 180°C (350°F/Gas Mark 4), or the bottom right oven in a four-door Aga, for 35–40 minutes. Sieve the icing sugar over the surface of the pud before serving it with either whipped cream or, better still, Vanilla Iced Cream (page 29).

Cinnamon Pancakes with Apple Fudgey Filling Served with Dark Chocolate Sauce (pages 75 and 92)

CINNAMON PANCAKES WITH APPLE FUDGEY FILLING SERVED WITH HOT CHOCOLATE SAUCE

These pancakes can be made and filled and frozen in their dish. Allow 3 hours at room temperature to thaw them. The nicer the apples you use for the filling, the nicer the pancakes will be – my favourite apples (both for eating and cooking) are Cox's, which make this an autumnal pudding.

SERVES 8
For the batter
150 g (5 oz) flour
10 ml (2 tsp) ground cinnamon
25 g (1 oz) caster sugar
25 g (1 oz) butter, melted
2 large eggs
300 ml (½ pint) milk
150 ml (¼ pint) water

For the filling
75 g (3 oz) butter
75 g (3 oz) soft light brown sugar
8 good eating apples, preferably Cox's, peeled, cored
  and chopped
grated rind of 1 lemon

To finish
15 ml (1 tbsp) icing sugar
Dark Chocolate Sauce (page 92), to serve

*F*irst make the batter. In a blender or food processor, whizz together all the batter ingredients until smooth. Let the mixture stand for about 1 hour, then make into pancakes, as thin as possible, as described in Cinnamon Pancakes with Chocolate Cream (page 72).

To make the filling, melt the butter in a saucepan and add the sugar. Cook for a minute or two, then add the chopped apples and lemon rind. Cook for 15–20 minutes, over a gentle heat, until soft and pulpy, stirring occasionally so that the apples cook evenly.

Butter a wide, shallow ovenproof dish. Put a spoonful of the apple mixture in the middle of each pancake, allowing 2 pancakes per person. Fold into triangular parcels, tucking the ends under. Arrange in the dish.

Just before serving, dust the pancakes with the icing sugar and put them into the oven pre-heated to 180°C (350°F/Gas Mark 4), or the bottom right oven in a four-door Aga, for 15 minutes. Serve warm, with the hot Dark Chocolate Sauce handed separately.

FINGER PUDDINGS

There are so many occasions when you find yourself short of time when entertaining, and want to round off a meal with something chocolatey yet don't have the time to make or serve a pudding as such. This is where chocolate goodies which can be eaten with the fingers with a cup of coffee are invaluable. They can be made ahead and stored in airtight containers, and all make a delicious finale to an otherwise rushed or hurried meal. The recipes for Chocolate Cups, using both white and dark chocolate, with a variety of fillings, are very decorative, for a minimum of effort.

CHOCOLATE FUDGE

I love the dense chocolate flavour of this fudge. So often I have found that chocolate fudge tastes too mildly of chocolate – this recipe is perfect for my taste!

900 g (2 lb) granulated sugar
225 g (8 oz) butter
397 g (14 fl oz) can condensed milk
400 ml (14 fl oz) whole milk
a few drops of vanilla essence
30 ml (2 tbsp) cocoa powder, sieved

Put all the ingredients into a heavy saucepan and stir over a moderate heat until the butter has melted and the sugar dissolved completely – there should be absolutely no gritty feeling under your wooden stirring spoon. Then bring the mixture to the boil, and boil until it reaches 250°F or 120°C on a sugar thermometer: another way of testing is to have a bowl or mug of cold water ready and to drop a dribble of hot fudge into the water. It should form a soft ball. The boiling time will take at least 5 minutes. (It is hard to be absolutely accurate because it does depend on how fast the boil is.) You don't need to stir all the time the fudge boils, just occasionally, but do beware of using a saucepan with too thin a base, as then the fudge will tend to stick and burn on the bottom.

While the fudge is boiling, butter a baking tray about 35 × 40 cm (14 × 16 inches) and about 4 cm (1 ½ inches) deep. When the fudge has reached the soft ball stage, remove the pan from the heat and stir until the fudge thickens, then pour and scrape it into the prepared baking tray. Leave to cool, then mark it into squares with a sharp knife. When the fudge is quite cold, cut up the squares and store in an airtight container. (By the way, fudge freezes beautifully, if you want to make a batch several weeks ahead.)

DARK AND WHITE CHOCOLATE-COATED FLORENTINES

These are so delicious to eat – they make a wonderful gift. Florentines are a mixture of dried fruit, cherries and nuts set in a toffee-like base, with a coating of chocolate on one side.

MAKES 16
90g (3½ oz) butter
100g (4oz) caster sugar
100g (4oz) flaked almonds, roughly chopped
25g (1oz) sultanas
25g (1oz) chopped mixed peel
8 glacé cherries, chopped
30ml (2tbsp) single cream
100g (4oz) dark chocolate
100g (4oz) white chocolate

Line three baking trays with non-stick baking parchment. Melt the butter in a saucepan over a gentle heat, then stir in the sugar, and heat gently until dissolved, then boil fast for 1 minute. Remove the pan from the heat and stir in the almonds, sultanas, mixed peel, cherries and cream. Mix all together thoroughly.

Drop evenly spaced teaspoonsful of the mixture on to the prepared baking trays (the mixture will spread as it cooks) and bake in the oven pre-heated to 180°C (350°C/Gas Mark 4), or the bottom right oven of a four-door Aga, for 10 minutes, until golden. Remove from the oven and push the edges of each biscuit into tidy rounds, using a palette knife. Leave to cool for a few minutes on the baking trays, then lift the biscuits carefully on to a wire rack, and leave to cool completely.

Meanwhile, break the dark and white chocolate into separate heatproof bowls set over saucepans of hot water (take care not to let the bottoms of the bowls touch the water) and heat very gently until melted. Be careful not to let the chocolate overheat. Coat one side of each biscuit with the melted chocolate, and as the chocolate begins to set on the biscuits, make a wavy pattern with a fork in the chocolate. You will have about 8 florentines coated in dark chocolate and 8 coated in white chocolate.

Store in an airtight tin, with a layer of greaseproof paper between each layer of florentines. Keep them in a cool place, but preferably not in the fridge, where I find that the chocolate takes on a sort of bloom. I don't advise you to freeze these biscuits – I tried once and they weren't a patch on freshly made ones.

Dark Chocolate Oatmeal Crisp Biscuits, Chocolate-Dipped Viennese Fingers, Chocolate Biscuit Squares, Florentines (pages 81-88)

White Chocolate Cups with Raspberry Cream and Raspberry Sauce (page 84)

WHITE CHOCOLATE CUPS WITH CANDY SPANDY AND BANANAS

This recipe is for those with an extremely sweet tooth. My father loves it, but it is verging on the sweet side even for me! Candy Spandy is caramelized condensed milk.

SERVES 24
For the chocolate cases
225 g (8 oz) white chocolate
30 ml (2 tbsp) single cream

For the filling
397 g (14 oz) can condensed milk, simmered
  unopened for 20 minutes, then cooled before opening
2 bananas
2.5 ml (½ tsp) vanilla essence

To finish (optional)
a little grated dark chocolate

*B*reak up the white chocolate into a heat-proof bowl set over a pan of hot water. Add the cream. Let the chocolate melt in the cream, then stir briefly just to blend. Remove the bowl from the heat and let it cool for few minutes before smoothing it round the sides and bases of 24 small paper cases. This is easiest done, I find, with a small palette knife. You will find the chocolate tends to slip down the sides, so try to smooth it up the sides as evenly as possible.

Leave the chocolate-lined cases in a cool place

before carefully tearing off the paper cases ready for filling.

Pour the condensed milk into a small non-stick saucepan and heat gently for 20 minutes, stirring all the time, until caramelized. Leave to cool.

A couple of hours before serving, chop the bananas and stir them into the caramelized milk with the vanilla essence. Spoon the mixture into the chocolate cases. If you like, sprinkle each with a little grated dark chocolate.

WHITE CHOCOLATE CUPS WITH RASPBERRY CREAM AND RASPBERRY SAUCE

These both look and taste good – the white chocolate cups with their filling of pink raspberry cream, served sitting in a puddle of raspberry sauce. You can make these with dark chocolate if you prefer, but I like them best made with white chocolate.

MAKES 12
For the chocolate cases
100 g (4 oz) white chocolate
30 ml (2 tbsp) single cream

For the raspberry cream and sauce
300 ml (½ pint) double cream
450 g (1 lb) raspberries
75 g (3 oz) icing sugar
mint sprigs

*B*reak up the chocolate into a heatproof bowl. Add the cream and set over a pan of hot water. Let the chocolate melt in the cream, then stir briefly just to blend. Let the chocolate cool for a few minutes, then smooth it round the sides and bases of 12 small paper cases. You will find the chocolate tends to slip down the sides – try to smooth it up the sides as far as possible. Leave in a cool place until set firm, then carefully peel off the paper cases.

Reserve a few well-shaped raspberries. Liquidize, then sieve the remaining raspberries with the icing sugar. Set aside for the sauce. Using a fork, mash the remaining raspberries and fold them into the whipped cream, whipped until fairly stiff. Fill the chocolate cases with the raspberry cream. Top each with the perfect raspberries and a mint sprigs. Serve on individual serving plates, sitting in a puddle of the raspberry sauce.

CHOCOLATE-DIPPED VIENNESE FINGERS

These delicious finger biscuits really do melt in your mouth, and they are enhanced by the ends of each biscuit being coated with dark chocolate. They make a good chocolate nibble with a cup of coffee, either by themselves, or as part of a selection of chocolate eats.

MAKES ABOUT 18
100 g (4 oz) dark chocolate
100 g (4 oz) butter
50 g (2 oz) icing sugar, sieved
100 g (4 oz) flour
1.2 ml (¼ tsp) baking powder
a few drops of vanilla essence

*P*ut 25 g (1 oz) of the chocolate into a heatproof bowl set over a saucepan of hot water (take care not to let the bottom of the bowl touch the water) and heat very gently until melted. Remove the bowl from the heat and stir the chocolate, then leave it to cool.

Meanwhile, cream the butter in a bowl, gradually adding the icing sugar. Beat until the mixture is pale and fluffy. Beat in the cooled chocolate, then the flour sifted with the baking powder, and the vanilla essence.

Butter 2 baking trays. Pipe the mixture, using a star nozzle, into 7.5 cm (3 inch) lengths on the prepared baking trays. Bake in the oven preheated to 180°C (350°C/Gas Mark 4), or the bottom right oven in a four-door Aga, for 15 minutes, until golden. Remove the biscuits from the oven and leave to cool for a minute on the baking trays, then carefully lift them on to wire racks. Leave to cool completely.

Melt the remaining chocolate in a heatproof bowl over a saucepan of hot water. Stir, then dip each end of each biscuit in the chocolate. Leave on the wire racks to set, then store in airtight containers, with greaseproof paper between each layer.

DARK CHOCOLATE TRUFFLES WITH ANGOSTURA BITTERS

These really are delicious. Most people associate rum or brandy with truffles, but the Angostura bitters work really well.

MAKES ABOUT 24-30
350 g (12 oz) dark chocolate
10 ml (2 tsp) instant coffee dissolved in 30 ml (2 tbsp) boiling water
175 g (6 oz) unsalted butter, diced
about 2.5 ml (½ tsp) Angostura bitters

*B*reak the chocolate into a heatproof bowl, and add the coffee liquid. Put the bowl over a saucepan of hot water, heat very gently until the chocolate has melted. Remove the bowl from the pan and beat in the butter, bit by bit. Beat in the Angostura bitters and leave the mixture in a cool place until quite firm.

Sieve the cocoa powder over a work surface and rub some cocoa between the palms of your hands. Take a teaspoonful of the chocolate mixture and roll into a ball between the palms of your hands. Roll in cocoa and put on a tray. Continue in the same way until all the chocolate mixture is used up.

Put the finished truffles in the fridge to firm up, then pack into containers, with a layer of greaseproof paper between each layer of truffles.

CHOCOLATE BISCUIT SQUARES

MAKES 20
225 g (8 oz) dark chocolate
225 g (8 oz) butter
60 ml (4 tbsp) brandy
12 digestive biscuits, crushed to crumbs
75 g (3 oz) glacé cherries, chopped
75 g (3 oz) walnuts, coarsely chopped, toasted then cooled
2 large eggs
75 g (3 oz) caster sugar

*B*utter a baking tray about 30 × 25 cm (10 × 12 inches) and about 2.5 cm (1 inch) deep. Break the chocolate into bits into a saucepan and add the butter cut into chunks. Melt over a gentle heat, then stir in the brandy, crushed biscuits, cherries and toasted walnuts.

Whisk the eggs, gradually adding the sugar. Whisk until very thick and pale. Fold together the egg and chocolate mixtures and pour into the prepared baking tray. Smooth out evenly and leave to set in a cool place for several hours. Mark and cut into 4 cm (2½ inch) squares. Store in an airtight container, with a piece of greaseproof paper between each layer, in the fridge.

Dark Chocolate Truffles with Angostura Bitters (page 86)

DARK CHOCOLATE OATMEAL CRISP BISCUITS

MAKES 16
175g (6oz) butter
100g (4oz) caster sugar
165g (5½oz) flour
40g (1½oz) cocoa powder
50g (2oz) porridge oats
a few drops of vanilla essence
50g (2oz) dark chocolate

Cream the butter in a bowl, gradually adding the sugar. Beat until the mixture is light and fluffy. Sift the flour and cocoa powder and mix into the cream mixture, then mix in the porridge oats and vanilla essence to make a fairly stiff dough.

Roll the dough out on a lightly floured work surface to the thickness of a 10p piece, and cut into circles about 5 cm (2 inches) in diameter. Bake on a baking tray in the oven pre-heated to 180°C (350°C/Gas Mark 4), or the bottom right oven of a four-door Aga, for 10–12 minutes. Remove the biscuits from the oven, leave them for a minute on the baking tray, then carefully lift them on to wire racks, using a palette knife. Leave to cool completely.

Break the chocolate into a small bowl. Set the bowl over a pan of simmering water and heat gently, stirring occasionally, until the chocolate has melted. Remove from the heat and dip in each biscuit to half-coat in chocolate then allow to dry on a wire rack. Store in an airtight tin.

DARK CHOCOLATE CUPS WITH GINGER CREAM

MAKES 12
For the chocolate cases
225g (8oz) dark chocolate

For the ginger cream
300ml (½pint) double cream
30ml (2tbsp) ginger wine
6 pieces of preserved ginger, drained and cut into slivers

Break the chocolate into a heatproof bowl and set over a pan of hot water until the chocolate melts. Stir briefly to mix, remove the chocolate from the heat and smooth it round the sides and bases of 12 small paper cake cases. (There is no need to let the chocolate cool for a few minutes, as with white chocolate.) Let the cases stand in a cool place until firm – about 15–20 minutes – then carefully peel off the paper cases. If you let them stand for several hours the chocolate becomes too hard and brittle; it is much easier to tear off the paper when they are just firm enough.

To make the ginger cream filling, whip the cream with the ginger wine until fairly stiff. Spoon the cream into the chocolate cases, or pipe it in, using a star nozzle, which looks prettier. Fill the cases about three-quarters full, then arrange a small cluster of slivered ginger in the middle of the cream on each cup.

DARK AND WHITE CHOCOLATE–DIPPED STRAWBERRIES

These really look most attractive arranged alternately on a plate. The strawberries must be in perfect condition, not at all mushy; and try to choose berries of as even a size as possible. To add to their appeal (to the eye!) leave on their leaves and stalks too, if possible. Don't keep them in the fridge as the chocolate takes on a bloom. They don't take a second to dip, but must be made the day they are to be eaten.

MAKES 24
50 g (2 oz) dark chocolate
50 g (2 oz) white chocolate
25 g (1 oz) butter

*B*reak the chocolates into separate heatproof bowls, set over saucepans of very hot water, and heat very gently for just long enough to melt the chocolates (take care that the bottom of the bowls do not touch the water). Remove from the heat and stir.

Have ready a baking tray lined with a piece of non-stick baking parchment. Dip half the number of strawberries into the dark chocolate, and the other half into the white chocolate, making sure each berry is well dipped. Lay them on the prepared baking tray and leave in a cool place until the chocolate has set.

DARK CHOCOLATE RICE CRISPIES

There are many versions of this traditional children's tea-time goodie, but this one is far and away the best, I think, and adults fall on them with cries of glee. I find myself making them when our two younger children are at school so that I can lick out the saucepan without having rivals for the treat! My sister Liv Milburn originally gave me this recipe.

MAKES 14-18
75 g (3 oz) dark chocolate
75 g (3 oz) butter
30 ml (2 tbsp) golden syrup (dip the spoon in boiling
water before measuring the syrup, that way it
slips easily off the spoon)
about 6-8 handfuls rice crispies

*M*elt the chocolate and the butter together in a saucepan over a gentle to moderate heat. Stir in the golden syrup and bubble gently for a minute or two, then add the rice crispies. Mix well together and remove the pan from the heat. Leave to cool in the pan for 10–15 minutes, stirring occasionally so that the crispies are evenly coated.

Put paper cake cases in bun tins and scoop the chocolate crispy mixture into the cases, using a teaspoon. Leave for several hours to cool and set. Store in an airtight container.

SAUCES

A sauce, either of a flavour complementary to chocolate or a chocolate sauce itself, adds a superb finishing touch to many chocolate puddings. In some cases it is an integral part of the pudding as with profiteroles (page 50) which would be really pretty dreary served without their accompanying chocolate sauce, and the Pears in Hot Chocolate Sauce recipe on page 76.

Dark chocolate sauce is a very useful item to keep stored in a screw-topped container in your fridge: it is so good warmed up and served with vanilla or coffee iced cream. The Coffee Cream Sauce on page 90 is a real chocolate pudding enhancer – I always serve it with the Dark Chocolate and Praline Terrine (page 13), and with a number of other puddings in this book.

COFFEE CREAM SAUCE

I do so love the flavours of chocolate and coffee together. This sauce sets off any chocolate pudding perfectly.

MAKES 600 ml (1 pint)
600 ml (1 pint) single cream
2.5 ml (½ tsp) cornflour
75 g (3 oz) caster sugar
4 large egg yolks
20 ml (3 tsp) good instant coffee

Heat the cream in a saucepan over a gentle to moderate heat, until just below boiling point. Meanwhile, whisk together the cornflour, sugar, egg yolks and coffee until well mixed. Pour on a little of the hot cream and mix well, then return to the pan containing the remaining cream and cook over a moderate heat, stirring continuously, until the sauce is thick enough to coat the back of the spoon – take care not to let it boil. Serve cold or warm.

If you intend to serve the sauce cold, or if it is to sit for any length of time, wring out a piece of greaseproof paper in water and cover the sauce with it – this prevents a skin from forming.

VANILLA CREAM SAUCE

This delicious sauce is a proper egg yolk-thickened vanilla custard sauce. It is a world apart from custard as we often think of it – that ochre-yellow, gluey-thick, oversweet stodge. This creamy, vanilla-fragrant sauce is so good served with chocolate puddings of all descriptions, particularly a hot chocolate soufflé – or if you wish, you can leave out the vanilla and substitute orange or lemon rind.

MAKES 600 ml (1 pint)
600 ml (1 pint) single cream
4 large egg yolks
75 g (3 oz) caster sugar
2.5 ml (½ tsp) cornflour
2.5 ml (½ tsp) vanilla essence

*P*ut the cream into a saucepan and heat, over a gentle to moderate heat, to just below boiling point. Meanwhile, whisk together the egg yolks, sugar, cornflour and vanilla essence, until really smooth. Pour on a little of the hot cream, mix well, then return to the pan containing the remaining hot cream. Stir over a moderate heat, until the sauce is thick enough to coat the back of your spoon – take care not to let it boil. Remove from the heat and serve warm.

If the sauce is to stand for any length of time, wring out a piece of greaseproof paper in water, and put it on top of the sauce as it sits in the pan – this prevents a skin from forming.

ORANGE SABAYON SAUCE

This sauce is delicious served with any chocolate and orange pudding, but I like it especially with the Steamed Chocolate Pudding on page 73. It will keep warm for up to 30 minutes in the top of a double boiler.

MAKES ABOUT 300 ml (½ pint)
juice of 4 large oranges, not less than 150 ml (¼ pint)
3 large egg yolks
50 g (2 oz) caster sugar

*P*ut all the ingredients into the top of a double boiler, and, over a moderate heat, whisk with a balloon whisk (not an electric hand-held whisk) until the sauce is thickened.

WHITE CHOCOLATE CREAM SAUCE

This sauce is rich and delicious, but a little goes a long way. I use it to serve with a dark chocolate mousse – really, I have to admit, for the sake of the appearance!

SERVES 6
175g (6oz) white chocolate
150ml (¼ pint) double cream

Break the chocolate into a heatproof bowl and add the cream. Set the bowl over a saucepan of hot water until the chocolate has melted in the cream. Mix together until smooth, then serve.

DARK CHOCOLATE SAUCE

This is an invaluable sauce to have stored away in a screw-topped jar in the fridge, ready to be heated up and served with all sorts of different puddings, or with iced creams, or fruit, especially pears or bananas. Chocolate sauces vary so much: the ones I abhor are those which are too milky or worse still, watery, tasting insufficiently of chocolate, and thin and dreary in texture. You can't say that about this one!

MAKES 300ml (½ pint)
175g (6oz) caster sugar
5ml (1 tsp) vanilla essence
45ml (3 tbsp) golden syrup (dip the spoon in boiling water before measuring the syrup, that way the syrup slips easily off the spoon)
90ml (6 tbsp) cocoa powder

Put all the ingredients together with 200 ml (7 fl oz) boiling water into a saucepan, and heat gently until the sugar is dissolved and the syrup is melted. Stir until smooth. Boil fast, for about 5 minutes. The more you boil this sauce, the fudgier it becomes.

The Finishing Touch
Chocolate Decorations

Dark Chocolate Rose Leaves

This is one of the prettiest and simplest ways to use chocolate decoratively, and I thought you would find it as useful as I do. It's very effective in particular as a decoration for the White Chocolate Mousse (page 9).

Pick several even-sized and well shaped rose leaves. Make sure they are absolutely clean and dry. Melt some dark chocolate in a bowl over a saucepan of hot water.

Lay a piece of non-stick baking parchment on a baking tray. Using a small palette knife, smear the melted chocolate evenly over the underside of each leaf, and lay them, chocolate side up, on the paper for several hours until quite cold. Then carefully peel off the leaf from the set chocolate, which will leave you with perfect chocolate leaves. Easy!

White chocolate leaves can be made in exactly the same way using white chocolate, and they look particularly good as a decoration for Iced Chocolate and Brandy Creams (page 30).

Chocolate Caraque

Break 100 g (4 oz) chocolate into pieces and put in a bowl over a pan of hot water. Heat gently, stirring, until the chocolate has melted. Pour it in a thin layer on to a marble slab and leave to set until it no longer sticks to the hand when touched. Holding a large knife with both hands, push the blade across the surface of the chocolate to roll pieces off in long curls.

93

CHOCOLATE TRIANGLES

*M*ake a sheet of chocolate as above and cut it into 6–8 triangles.

CHOCOLATE SQUARES

*M*ake a sheet of chocolate as above and cut into 2.5 cm (1 inch) squares.

CHOCOLATE CIRCLES

*M*ake a sheet of chocolate as above and stamp out circles using a small round cutter.

CHOCOLATE CURLS

*U*sing a potato peeler, 'peel' thin layers straight from the block of chocolate.

CRYSTALLIZED FLOWERS AND PETALS

1 egg white
leaves, flowers or petals such as mint leaves, violets, primroses and rose petals
caster sugar

*W*hisk the egg white lightly. Paint both sides of the leaves, flowers or petals with egg white and then sprinkle both sides with caster sugar. Shake off surplus sugar and leave to dry. If necessary, sprinkle a second time with sugar to ensure they are evenly coated. Leave to dry completely before storing in a screw-top jar.

INDEX

macaroon, chocolate and, mousse, 16
marrons glacé: chocolate and
    marrons glacé iced cream, 29
meringue: baked spiced chocolate
    meringue pudding, 76
    cherry and chocolate meringue
        gâteau, 24
    chocolate and chestnut cream
        meringue, 20, *22*
    chocolate meringues with rum-
        whipped cream, 26, *27*
    coffee, chocolate and almond
        meringue gâteau, 21, *23*
    hazelnut meringue with chocolate
        cream, 25
    vanilla and chocolate cream
        pavlova, 18, *19*
mocha mousse, 17
mousses: chocolate and amaretto
    macaroon, 16
    chocolate mousse cake, *2*, 48–9
    chocolate and orange, 10, 12
    chocolate and peppermint, 12–13
    mocha, 17
    white chocolate, 9, *11*

nègre en chemise, 49
Nesselrose pudding, 33, *34*

oatmeal crisp biscuits, *82*, 88
orange: chocolate and orange
    cake, 37

chocolate and orange mousse,
    10, 12
chocolate profiteroles with orange
    cream, 50, *51*
orange and chocolate Bavarian
    cream, 14, *15*
orange and lemon iced cream, 30
orange and lemon roulade, *55*, 56
orange sabayon sauce, 91

pancakes, cinnamon, 72–3, *78*, 79
pavlova, 18, *19*
pears with hot chocolate sauce, 76–7
pecan pie, *63*, 64
peppermint: chocolate and
    peppermint crisp iced cream, 28
    chocolate and peppermint mousse,
        12–13
petit pots au chocolat, 69, *70*
praline: dark chocolate and praline
    terrine, 7, *13*
profiteroles, 50, *51*
prunes: chocolate roulade with prune
    and Armagnac cream, 53

raisins: rich chocolate, raisin and rum
    iced cream, 32, *35*
raspberries: chocolate crisp roulade
    with, 57
    white chocolate cups with, *83*,
        84–5
rice crispies, 89

rice pudding, 74, *75*
rose leaves, 93
roulades: chocolate and apricot, 58
    chocolate and coffee, 52–3, *54*
    chocolate crisp, 57
    chocolate with prune and
        Armagnac cream, 53
    orange and lemon, *55*, 56

Sachertorte, 38, *39*
sauces: chocolate, 76–7
    coffee cream, 90
    dark chocolate, 92
    orange sabayon, 91
    vanilla cream, 91
    white chocolate cream, 92
soufflé, hot chocolate and coffee,
    16–17
steamed chocolate pudding, 73
strawberries, dark and white
    chocolate-dipped, *62*, 89

terrine, dark chocolate and praline,
    7, *13*
truffles with Angostura bitters, 86, *87*

vanilla: chocolate and vanilla
    cornflour pudding, 74
    vanilla and chocolate cream
        pavlova, 18, *19*
    vanilla cream sauce, 91
    vanilla iced cream, 29
Viennese fingers, *82*, 85